Catholic
Answers
to Catholic
Questions

Catholic Answers to Catholic Questions

Paul Thigpen, Ph.D.
Father Ray Ryland, Ph.D., J.D.
Father Francis Hoffman, J.C.D.

Our Sunday Visitor Publishing Division
Our Sunday Visitor, Inc.
Huntington, Indiana 46750

Nihil Obstat: Msgr. Michael Heintz, Ph.D.
Censor Librorum
Imprimatur: ✠ Bishop Kevin C. Rhoades
Bishop of Fort Wayne-South Bend
April 9, 2010

The *Nihil Obstat* and *Imprimatur* are official declarations that a book or pamphlet is free of doctrinal or moral error. No implication is contained therein that those who have granted the *Nihil Obstat* or *Imprimatur* agree with the contents, opinions, or statements expressed.

Our Sunday Visitor Publishing Division
Our Sunday Visitor, Inc.
200 Noll Plaza
Huntington, IN 46750
1-800-348-2440
bookpermissions@osv.com

ISBN: 978-1-59276-636-9 (Inventory No. T918)
LCCN: 2010924067

Cover design by Rebecca J. Heaston
Cover images: Shutterstock
Interior design by Sherri L. Hoffman

PRINTED IN THE UNITED STATES OF AMERICA

Contents

"The Catholic Answer Man"

"The Catholic Answer Man." That's the nickname some of my friends have given me, because I seem to spend most of my waking hours answering questions about the Catholic faith. It's not a role I've sought out. But folks know that as a convert to the Faith and a theology professor, I've already had to answer for myself many of the same questions they ask. And when I don't have the answers, as is often the case, I usually know where to look for them.

The queries come from my college students, fellow parishioners, close friends, people I encounter briefly at social gatherings, and even total strangers who write or e-mail me from around the world.

The greatest number of questions I field, however, come from two sources: First, the readers of *The Catholic Answer* (affectionately known as *TCA*), a national bimonthly magazine for which I served as editor. Second, visitors to the *TCA Question of the Day*, an online Q&A that appears at the Web site of our parent publishing company, Our Sunday Visitor, Inc. (www.osv.com).

The mission of these two publications is quite focused — to answer queries about all things Catholic. But to fulfill such a mission, our staff of editors and contributors must range across a remarkably wide array of topics: Scripture, theology, the Church, the sacraments, spirituality, liturgy, morality, history, apologetics, and much more.

Our labors have resulted, I trust, in a wider, deeper, clearer understanding of the Catholic faith for our readers. It has certainly done so for us. I must admit: with three theological degrees, including a Ph.D., I've nevertheless learned more about the Catholic faith on the job with *TCA* than I could ever have imagined during my years of formal study. No doubt the rest of the *TCA* team would say the same.

Our energetic readers have kept us amply supplied with a steady stream of questions that have been in turn familiar, surprising, fascinating, provocative, skeptical, significant, merely curious, urgent, and agonizing. In response, we've labored long and hard to provide them with answers.

This book is a collection of Q&As gathered from the past six and a half years of *TCA* (May/June 2003 through November/December 2009) and the past two years of the *TCA Question of the Day* (July 2007 through August 2009).

Over the years our team has collaborated on these projects, I've come to feel especially grateful for the expertise, talent, hard work, and gracious collegiality of Father Ray Ryland, J.D., Ph.D., and Father Francis Hoffman, J.C.D. Father Ryland has written our "*TCA* Faith" column; and Father Hoffman, our "*TCA* Life" column. In this book, each contributor is identified by his initials at the end of the answer he has provided: RR for Father Ryland, FH for Father Hoffman, and PT for myself.

From the magazine and the online Q&A, we had enough material to fill five volumes or more. So we've had to be quite selective about the ones included here. Two criteria shaped our choices.

First, we wanted the questions to reflect all the various categories of subject matter reflected in the magazine. In this book they have been arranged by chapter according to these topics.

And second, we've tried to avoid using Q&As that, while important, would simply repeat information available in many other places: queries about the origins of the Rosary, for example, or how a pope is elected. Instead, we've chosen for this collection answers that are less accessible elsewhere; answers to questions we've not seen asked elsewhere; or answers that reflect certain distinctive insights of our team of contributors, given their particular backgrounds and expertise.

Because of these criteria, this book has a wide range of topics, but it's not intended as a comprehensive manual of answers for every important Catholic question. Instead, we believe you'll find here an informative, intriguing, stimulating, challenging, perhaps even life-changing selection of *Catholic Answers to Catholic Questions* not quite like any other.

Finally, we want to express our gratitude to our readers. Your thirst to know more about your Faith — and about Our Lord, who stands at the center of that Faith — is what drives our publications and led to the creation of this book. We're inspired by your quest for understanding, and we hope you'll keep sending us your questions.

Let's keep digging deeper — there's so much to learn!

— *Paul Thigpen*

1.

Questions about Scripture

Q. Do we have any of the original manuscripts of the books of the Bible?

A. No. The books of the Bible are so ancient, and were hand-copied so many times over the centuries, that all we have surviving are copies of copies of copies. In no case do we have what some would call the *autograph* of a book — that is, the original copy, such as one of the actual letters that was penned by the apostle Paul.

Think how priceless — both materially and spiritually — even one of these original manuscripts would be. So why did God allow them all to be lost?

According to one speculation, God knew that people would be tempted not just to venerate but to idolize the original manuscripts if we had them in our possession. So He has kept them from us. But only the Lord himself knows for sure His reasons for allowing them all to be lost.

— PT

Q. Are we always to take all Bible verses personally? In other words, when God says something to a person we're reading about in the Bible, are we to interpret that passage to mean that He is also speaking to us?

A. Sometimes, yes, the words spoken by God to a person in the Bible are intended for us as well in a direct manner. As an Old Testament example, consider the Ten Commandments. When God told Moses and the ancient Israelites, "You shall not steal"

(Ex 20:15), He was speaking to all people of all time. In the New Testament, when Jesus Christ, God in the flesh, told His listeners, "Love your enemies" (Mt 5:44), again, He was speaking to us all.

Nevertheless, we can't simply assume that everything spoken by God to someone in Scripture is spoken directly to us as well. For example: God told Abraham to kill his son Isaac and offer him as a sacrifice (see Gen 22:1-19). Even though this was only a test of faith and God didn't allow Abraham to actually carry it out, we shouldn't read this passage and take it to mean that God is putting us to a similar test or that He wants us to sacrifice our children.

At the same time, even a story like this can be read, if we do it carefully, in such a way that we learn a general *principle* behind what God was saying, which we can apply to our own lives. In the case of Abraham and Isaac, the obvious principle is that we must not value any attachment, even to our children, more than we value God. But even when attempting to discern principles, we must ask what differences in circumstances there may be between the scriptural situation and our own, which may determine the nature of our application.

Catholic tradition teaches us that some things Jesus commanded as recorded in the Gospels are for everyone who would embrace the Gospel; these are called the *evangelical precepts*. Others, however, which are more difficult to obey, are directed to those who "would be perfect"; they are called the *evangelical counsels*, or *counsels of perfection*.

The precepts have to do with matters of spiritual and moral necessity: "You shall love your neighbor as yourself" (Mt 22:39).

The counsels are voluntarily accepted by those who seek to move as quickly as possible toward the final goal of perfection to which everyone is called: "*If you would be perfect*, go, sell what you possess and give to the poor" (Mt 19:21, emphasis added). The apostle Paul offered a similar counsel — celibacy — which he made clear was not a "command of the Lord" to be obeyed by all Christians (see 1 Cor 7:25-35).

So how do we tell the difference between divine commands addressed only to someone in Scripture and those that are spoken to us directly as well? We need the interpretative tradition of the Church. That's why we must read Scripture "with the mind of the Church." The Bible alone isn't sufficient; it needs an authoritative interpreter.

— PT

Q. Why do some Bibles have upper-case references to God, while others have lower-case references? In other words, why do some use "he" or "him" or "his" instead of "He" or "Him" or "His"?

A. Capitalizing pronouns referring to God seems to many readers (including myself) an expression of reverence. For this reason, a number of Catholic and other Christian book and magazine publishers long ago adopted the practice.

However, historically speaking, capitalization is a relatively recent development in typography. The ancient manuscripts of the Bible were written in Hebrew, Greek, and Aramaic alphabets that did not have, at that time, distinct uppercase and lowercase letters. By the time Scripture was translated completely into English, our language had both uppercase and lowercase letters, but the oldest English Bibles, such as the (Catholic) Douay-Rheims and the (Protestant) King James (or Authorized) Versions, did not capitalize personal pronouns referring to the Deity.

Some later translations, such as the (Protestant) New American Standard Bible, adopted the practice of capitalizing pronouns referring to God. Doing so certainly has the practical advantage of eliminating ambiguity. For example, when a passage involves both God and a man, you can know instantly which one is referred to by a personal pronoun, simply by its uppercase or lowercase letter.

Nevertheless, trends in publishing tend to favor fewer capitalized words of any sort. Take a look at a photo of the Declaration of Independence, for example, and notice all the nouns capitalized in eighteenth-century English that we would not normally capitalize today.

In any case, most Bible translations today don't capitalize personal pronouns referring to God.

— *PT*

Q. In the Bible, the word "Lord," used in reference to God, is sometimes written as "Lord" and at other times as "LORD." For example, Psalm 8:2 (NAB) says: "O LORD, our Lord, how awesome is your name through all the earth!" Is there a difference between "LORD" and "Lord"?

A. The simple answer is that in classical Hebrew (the original language of the Psalms and, indeed, most of the Old Testament), they are two quite different words. The first is the proper noun representing God's personal name, as He revealed it to the ancient Jews, and the second is the more common name for God.

God's personal name was so highly revered that Jews refrained from speaking it aloud for fear of breaking the commandment against taking it in vain. Instead, the word *Adonai*, an intensive form of the common noun meaning "lord, master, sovereign," was substituted, even when God's name appeared in Scripture being read aloud. (Today, many orthodox Jews still refrain from writing or speaking the word "God," writing instead "G-d" and substituting for it such terms as "the Lord" or "the Almighty" in speech.)

The *Septuagint,* an ancient Greek translation of the Hebrew Scriptures used by Greek-speaking Jews throughout the world (and by the early Christians), made the same kind of substitution, using the Greek term for "lord" (*kyrios*).

Over the generations, though the written form of God's personal name was preserved in the Hebrew scriptural text, the original pronunciation was eventually forgotten because it was almost never spoken. Since ancient Hebrew had written characters only for consonant sounds (the vowels were supplied by oral tradition), all we know for certain is that this name is represented by four Hebrew letters that are transliterated in contemporary English as YHWH. This most holy name of God is thus commonly known as "the Tetragrammaton" (literally, "that which has four letters").

Whenever YHWH appears in the Hebrew text, English translators have often followed the Jewish tradition by rendering the word as "LORD," but they place it in small capital letters to indicate that it refers to God's personal name. When the term "Lord" appears in normal type, the Hebrew word translated is usually *Adonai* or some related common-noun form such as *adon*.

In the scriptural text you cited (Ps 8:2), "LORD" translates YHWH (the proper noun of God's personal name) and "Lord" translates *adon* (the common noun describing His sovereignty). This line could also be rendered: "O YHWH, our Sovereign, how awesome is your name through all the earth!" (See also v. 10.)

An exception to this custom in translation was necessary when the original Hebrew text referred to God as *Adonai* YHWH, "the Lord YHWH." Rather than translate the phrase awkwardly as "the Lord LORD," it was often rendered instead as "the Lord GOD" — with the small capital letters in "GOD," once again, denoting that the Tetragrammaton was indicated.

As an interesting aside: The Jewish scholarly tradition finally developed a system of characters to represent vowels, which were then inserted into the ancient biblical text of consonants. But to remind the reader of Scripture that God's most holy personal name, YHWH, was not to be spoken, the custom arose of inserting the vowels from the term *Adonai* into the consonants of YHWH. In earlier English, the Tetragrammaton was typically transliterated as JHVH rather than YHWH. The translators of some early English Bibles, such as the King James Version, then used the supplied vowels along with the consonants as given in the divine Name.

The result? *YHWH* was rendered as "Jehovah," which actually has no real basis in the original text. Modern scholars sometimes render *YHWH* as "Yahweh," and this term has spilled over into some contemporary songs. But "Yahweh" is really just another guess at the original pronunciation.

— PT

Q. Why doesn't the Bible talk about dinosaurs, especially in the creation story in Genesis?

A. There are many things in the natural world that the Bible doesn't talk about — not just the dinosaur, but also the kangaroo, the turkey, the duck-billed platypus, and a host of other animals, many of which are still with us.

Why not? First, a book attempting to speak of every creature on earth — and especially every creature that has ever been on earth — would run to countless volumes. More importantly, knowledge of these things is not necessary for our salvation.

As for dinosaurs, keep in mind that the word "dinosaur," meaning "terrible lizard," was coined in 1842 by the English paleontologist Sir Richard Owen. If any biblical passage written in ancient times does, in fact, refer to a dinosaur, it would do so with a different term used by ancient people.

Some have speculated that the "great sea monsters" cited in several biblical passages (for example, Gen 1:21) might have included aquatic dinosaurs. Scripture also speaks of a great sea monster that it calls "Leviathan" (see, for example, Ps 74:14). Others have suggested that biblical references to "dragons" should be understood as dinosaurs (see, for example, Pss 74:13 and 91:13; Is 27:1).

In any case, we can note that when the Book of Genesis tells us God created "all kinds of living creatures," the dinosaurs are no doubt included (Gen 1:24; also v. 20). The human author of the text may not have known about the prehistoric existence of dinosaurs, but the Divine Author certainly did.

— PT

Q. In the Old Testament, the descendants of each son of the patriarch Jacob (Israel) were considered a tribe, carrying that son's name. All, that is, except for Joseph. But there are "half-tribes" mentioned. Are the half-tribes of Israel related to Joseph?

A. Yes. According to the biblical account, the descendants of each of Joseph's eleven brothers became a tribe that carried the brother's name: Reuben, Simeon, Levi, Judah, Dan, Naphtali, Gad, Asher, Issachar, Zebulun, and Benjamin (see Gen 29:31–30:24 and 35:16-18). Joseph himself had two sons, Ephraim and Manasseh.

Joseph's father, Jacob (Israel), blessed these two grandsons on his deathbed — adopting them as his own sons, saying that Joseph's descendants would be known by their names, and prophesying that the descendants of both sons would be numerous. Thus, the two resulting "half-tribes" were known as Ephraim and Manasseh; eventually they came to be recognized fully as "tribes" (see Gen 48:5-6, 19; Num 1:33, 35; 32:33, 34:14).

— PT

Q. Do we have any examples of humor in the Bible?

A. Forms of humor differ widely from culture to culture. For that reason, ancient Near-Eastern humor may not leave us in stitches but, if we understand it, we can see that there is humor in the Scripture. Ancient texts sometimes confront us with an incongruity intended to be humorous. Irony and hyperbole (exaggeration) are especially prominent aspects of such humor.

For example, the humorous incongruity in the Book of Genesis, when Abraham bargained with God to spare the city of Sodom (Gen 18:17-33), is unmistakable. Here we find the almighty Creator of the universe haggling with a mere mortal, as if they were a couple of street-savvy merchants in a roadside bazaar. Sly old Abe keeps upping the ante and, in the end, the mere mortal walks away with the bargain!

Or think of the scene in the Book of Numbers, where the pagan prophet Balaam receives a divine rebuke from his pack animal (Num 22:21-35). Not only is there an element of slapstick here when the donkey starts talking, but the story is also full of laughable irony: the normally dumb critter speaks, while the prophet acts asinine!

— PT

Q. In the Bible, somewhere, it talks about people who made fun of a bald man. What happened to them?

A. You probably have in mind the account in 2 Kings 2:23-24. It describes how, when the prophet Elisha was out on the highway walking between two cities, a mob of boys came out of the city and approached him, shouting, "Go up, baldhead!"

Apparently, Elisha was being threatened with physical harm; their jeer was likely the equivalent of saying, "You'd better start running, baldie!" But the prophet "cursed them in the name of the Lord." They were immediately attacked by two she-bears who appeared out of the woods and "tore forty-two of the children to pieces."

— PT

Q. Where in the Bible does it say, "God laughed"?

A. Several Psalms in the Bible speak of God laughing at the wicked, because He is amused by the foolishness of mere human beings thinking that they can defy Him and ultimately get away with it. For example: "The wicked plot against the just and grind their teeth at them; but the Lord laughs at them, knowing their day is coming" (Ps 37:12-13). (See also Pss 2:4 and 59:8.)

— PT

Q. In Matthew 12:1-4, Jesus refers to "the bread of the Presence." Is this the same as the transubstantiated Presence and Essence of God? Didn't Our Lord transubstantiate bread into His Body for the very first time at the Last Supper? In other words, is the "bread of the Presence" the same as the Real Presence?

A. In that passage or its parallel in Mark 2:25-26, Our Lord is making a reference to the Old Testament account found in 1 Samuel 21:1-6. The bread in that account is the loaves baked weekly by the priests, then placed in the tabernacle or Ark of the Covenant, where they would lie in the "presence" of God (thus, "bread of the Presence").

At the end of the week, this bread would be replaced by new loaves, and only the priests could eat the old ones, because they had been made sacred by their time in the tabernacle. The term "Presence," then, refers to God's presence with regard to both the Old Testament bread and the Blessed Sacrament. But the two breads do not mean at all the same thing.

The former was sacred bread, consecrated for a special role in temple worship — but still only bread. It was called "bread of the Presence" simply because it had been made holy by lying in the Presence of God as He manifested himself in the Ark of the Covenant, or tabernacle, in Old Testament times. It was an offering; in fact, the NAB calls it "bread of offering."

The Eucharist, on the other hand, is, of course, the very Body and Blood, Soul and Divinity, of Our Lord himself. God is really, truly *present* in the Host in a unique way.

It is true that Eucharistic transubstantiation took place first on the night Our Lord was betrayed, and never before then. We might, however, view the Old Testament bread of the Presence as a symbolic foreshadowing of the Eucharist, as was the manna that was kept in the Ark of the Covenant, or the unleavened bread at the Passover meal each year.

— *PT*

Q. Why do Catholics and Protestants number the Ten Commandments differently?

A. Though Catholics and Protestants agree that God gave Moses ten commandments, not everyone numbers them the same way. The Scripture itself makes no explicit division or enumeration of these commandments. Their division into verses in our modern Bibles — as with the entire system of scriptural chapters and verses — is, of course, not found in the original text; that organizational system was added in the Middle Ages.

The Catholic system, laid out by St. Augustine in the fifth century, was followed by Martin Luther, a central leader in the Protestant Reformation. To this day most Lutherans, following his lead, number the Ten Commandments the same way Catholics do. So this is not essentially a Catholic-Protestant disagreement.

Nevertheless, Protestants in the traditions stemming from the Church of England and the Reform leaders in Switzerland (John Calvin, Ulrich Zwingli) adopted a different way of numbering them.

To understand the differences, let's take a closer look at the scriptural texts involved and the history of numbering the commandments.

The divine commands given to Moses that we call the "Ten Commandments" (also the *Decalogue*) are recorded twice in the Old Testament, once in Exodus (20:1-17) and once in Deuteronomy (5:6-21). The two lists are almost identical, though their ordering is slightly different with regard to prohibitions against coveting.

The differences in numbering the commandments begin with the first one. In the arrangement used by Catholics, the first commandment is concerned broadly with false worship. The "other gods" (Deut 5:7) of the pagan peoples, which God forbade the ancient Israelites to worship, were typically represented by a "graven image" (v. 8). So it's logical not to divide these two statements into separate commandments, but rather to see them as a single prohibition of idolatry.

According to this way of numbering, then, the precept against taking the Lord's name in vain (Deut 5:11) is the second commandment; the injunction to keep the Sabbath (5:12) is third; and so on. The two final commands against coveting (5:21) are numbered separately, according to the order given in Deuteronomy: the ninth commandment forbids coveting a neighbor's wife, and the tenth forbids coveting a neighbor's property.

Though both these commands have to do with coveting, it certainly makes sense to separate them, because a neighbor's wife isn't in the same class as his property. This ordering recognizes that sins against things differ fundamentally from sins against persons. (It's true that servants are persons, but in this context, the desire for another person's servants seems to be not a lust to have sex with them, but rather a coveting of their productivity as financial assets.)

Adultery and theft belong to two different categories of immoral conduct, so the same must be said of the desire to commit these sins.

In the second system (which is more commonly used in contemporary American culture), the injunctions against having other gods and making graven images are considered separate commandments (the first and the second). The injunction against taking God's name in vain is thus viewed as the third commandment, and so on. Then, both commands against coveting are grouped together as one, ordered according to the list in Exodus list rather than the one in Deuteronomy.

Like the first way of numbering, this one is also ancient, having been used by the first-century Jewish historian Josephus, the third-century Christian theologian Origen, and others. Eastern Orthodox Christians typically follow this enumeration as well.

Interestingly enough, in the only place where Scripture refers specifically to these statements of God as being ten in number (Ex 34:28), they aren't called commandments. Literally translated, the Hebrew text speaks instead of ten "words" or "sayings" (see the RSV note on this passage).

With this in mind, we can see how the Jewish people, to whom the Commandments were originally given, have tradition-ally numbered them in yet a third way. In this enumeration, the first "word" is not a commandment at all, but rather the begin-ning declaration, "I, the Lord, am your God, who brought you out of the land of Egypt" (Ex 20:2; Deut 5:6).

— PT

Q. In the Old Testament (Lev 11:1-47; Deut 14:3-21), some animals are listed as unclean and therefore not to be eaten. What is the position of the Catholic Church on eating the "unclean" animals named in the Bible?

A. The Old Testament dietary laws had important functions. Among other things, they limited the social interaction of the ancient Jews with pagan peoples, which would typically have taken place around the meal table. Those who didn't observe the laws served "unclean" dishes in their homes, so the Jews couldn't share meals with them.

As a result, following these laws provided at least a partial shield against the bad influences of neighbors who practiced idol-atry and certain immoral practices connected to such worship, such as child sacrifice and ritual prostitution in pagan temples.

Once the Son of God became Man, however, the rationale for this separation ended among Christians. Christ's Church was to be universal, including both Jews and Gentiles (non-Jews). As St. Paul observed: "For there is no distinction between Jew and Greek; the same Lord is Lord of all and bestows his riches upon all who call upon him" (Rom 10:12).

For this reason, Jesus himself declared all foods to be clean (see Mk 7:14-23). The Church later did the same (see Acts 10).

— PT

Q. Many place names in the Old and New Testaments begin
with "Beth" — Bethlehem, Bethany, Bethsaida, and so on.
Does "Beth" have a particular significance in Hebrew?

A. The word "Beth" in Hebrew means "house." "Bethlehem"
means "house of bread." (How appropriate for the birthplace of
Jesus Christ, who called himself the "Bread of Life" [see Jn 6:48].)
"Bethsaida" means "house of fishing." "Bethany" means, according to some scholars, "house of misery," though others think it
derives from the Hebrew for "house of dates."

— *PT*

Q. Which of the four Gospels was written first?

A. The matter is quite complicated because scholars base their
various theories about which Gospel is prior on certain features
of the four texts that can be interpreted in contradicting ways.
Nearly all biblical scholars agree that Luke was not written first
and that John was written last, but the chief argument is whether
Matthew or Mark came first.

The "Matthew first" hypothesis dates all the way back to
St. Augustine in the fourth century. It's the oldest explanation,
following the order in which the Gospels appear in the canon,
and it's the one that was generally accepted by Catholics until
the mid-twentieth century. This hypothesis still has some support among scholars. The opposing hypothesis is that Mark, the
shortest Gospel, was written first.

In particular, there is considerable overlap in material among
the three Synoptic Gospels, as they are called (Matthew, Mark,
and Luke). So one or more of the Evangelists (Gospel authors)
most likely drew some of the material for their composition from
one of the others, to which they added their own unique material.
In addition, they may have drawn from another source that was
known to all of them.

If we could figure out who borrowed from whom, we'd have

a better idea of the order in which the books were written. Since Mark is the shortest Gospel, did Matthew and Luke draw from him in composing their Gospels, adding to it from other sources? Or did Mark draw from Matthew, condensing his material?

The truth is that none of the many scholarly hypotheses proposed to sort out the relationships between these Gospels — not just the order in which they were written, but also who borrowed from whom — is fully satisfactory. Each one fails to account for some feature of the four texts that have come down to us.

We should note that those who claim Mark is the first Gospel written may offer various kinds of textual evidence, but usually there is also an ideological factor involved as well — namely, an anti-Catholic influence. This has been pointed out by Catholic scholars and by some non-Catholic scholars as well.

If advocates of the position that Mark came first can establish their case, they can and do argue that the Matthew, chapter 16, passages about St. Peter and the Petrine primacy are not part of the earliest tradition but were added later.

The fact is, however, that even apart from Matthew 16, the entire weight of the rest of the New Testament confirms the role of Peter and his successors as earthly heads of the Church.

— PT and RR

Q. Why are St. John the Evangelist and his Gospel symbolized by an eagle?

A. The Old Testament Book of Ezekiel and the New Testament Book of Revelation both contain visions of an angelic creature with four faces (see Ezek 1:1-14; Rev 4:7). These four figures are known as the "Tetramorphs" (literally, "four forms"), and they include a man, a lion, an ox (or calf), and an eagle. As early as the second century, Christians were finding in these visions a symbolic representation of the four Evangelists: Matthew, Mark, Luke, and John.

Various arrangements were proposed to match each figure with a particular Evangelist. But the arrangement that finally prevailed in the Latin Church consisted in symbolizing St. Matthew by a man, St. Mark by a lion, St. Luke by an ox (or calf), and St. John by an eagle.

Several explanations have been offered for these associations. One has to do with the way each Gospel begins. Matthew starts with Christ's human genealogy. Mark begins with St. John the Baptist crying out in the wilderness as a lion roars in the desert. Luke starts his account in the temple, where oxen were sacrificed by the priests. And John's Gospel begins by soaring in the heavens like an eagle (Jn 1:1).

The four figures can also remind us of four aspects of Our Lord's nature and ministry: His humanity (man); His divinity (eagle); His kingship (lion); and His priesthood (ox).

— PT

Q. When Mary and Joseph had to travel from Nazareth to Bethlehem to pay their taxes, how long would the trip have taken them?

A. The distance "as the crow flies" from Nazareth to Bethlehem is about seventy miles. Under normal circumstances, without too many winding roads or rough spots to traverse, people might well have been able to travel (on foot or by donkey) about twenty miles a day, for a total one-way trip of perhaps four days. However, we must keep in mind several factors that would most likely have made the trip last much longer.

First, the land of Samaria lay along the most direct route between Nazareth and Bethlehem, and in Jesus' day, there was considerable hostility between Jews and Samaritans. Even if — as I think we can assume — Our Lady and St. Joseph bore no animosity toward Samaritans, it would have been difficult and even dangerous for them to travel through that country. They might have been harassed and would almost certainly have been refused lodging, just as Jesus and His disciples were treated some years later (see Lk 9:51-56).

Surely St. Joseph would have sought to protect his wife from such a threat. So, as was common among the Jews of the day, the holy couple would probably have journeyed far off the "direct" route to avoid Samaria, taking a detour from Galilee across the Jordan River and then back again into Judea farther south. That would have added many miles, and several days, to the journey.

Second, remember that Mary was close to the end of her pregnancy. No doubt they had to travel much more slowly than normal to avoid excessive discomfort for her and risks to the health of both mother and Child.

Given these factors, my guess is that the one-way trip took at least a week or ten days, and perhaps much longer.

— PT

Q. Scripture says that St. Joseph was alerted in a dream to take Jesus and Mary to Egypt before Herod murdered the Holy Innocents (boys under the age of two). How did St. John the Baptist escape the Massacre of the Innocents? Weren't he and Jesus about the same age?

A. St. John was indeed Our Lord's kinsman and would have been only a few months older. We have no record of his childhood, but it's a reasonable speculation that he and the young Jesus would have known each other and perhaps spent time together, given their kinship. A number of artists have, in fact, depicted the two children together, as in Leonardo da Vinci's *Virgin of the Rocks*.

As for his escape from Herod's slaughter of the Holy Innocents, St. Peter of Alexandria (d. 311) speculated that, to be spared the wicked king's wrath, the young John was taken into the desert, where he lived until many years later, when he came preaching repentance (see Mk 1:2-4). But St. Jerome, one of the first great biblical scholars, considered this an unlikely conjecture.

We must keep in mind that Scripture tells us Herod "ordered the massacre of all boys *in Bethlehem and its vicinity* two years old and under" (Mt 2:16, emphasis added). The massacre didn't extend to all the king's realm. John was born when his parents lived in an unnamed "town of Judah" that was "in the hill country" (Lk 1:39). We need not assume that this town was in the vicinity of Bethlehem, or that John's life was ever in danger.

— *PT*

Q. **Why didn't St. John the Baptist perform miracles? If he came "in the spirit and power of Elijah" (Lk 1:17), then why didn't he work miracles as Elijah did? (The Scripture says, "John performed no sign" [see Jn 10:41].)**

A. I don't know that the Church has ever spoken authoritatively on this issue, so I'll venture my own speculation. The miracles Jesus worked, Scripture tells us, were signs intended to direct people's attention to Jesus himself. They gave testimony to His divinity. When the apostles and other followers of Jesus worked miracles, these, too, were signs — pointing, not to the apostles, but to the Lord Jesus whom they preached.

With John, however, we have a situation in which many people had already concluded, before Jesus' public appearance in ministry, that the Baptist was himself the Messiah. He had to deny that notion publicly and point to Jesus instead (see Jn 1:15, 19-27).

Even then, some people continued to elevate John to a super-human status. After he was beheaded by Herod, some claimed that Jesus was the Baptist come back from the dead (see Mt 14:2; Lk 9:19). We also have historical evidence suggesting that some of John's followers did not take their cue from him about embracing Jesus as the "Lamb of God, who takes away the sins of the world" (Jn 1:29), but instead went on to develop a separate religious sect that considered John its founder.

John's primary role, of course, was precisely to serve as a sign —

to point others to the Lamb of God. But God had him perform that role through his compelling preaching and personal example rather than through miracles. Even without performing miracles, then, John constantly ran the risk of being mistaken for Christ or being followed instead of Christ. Think how much worse the situation would have been if he had performed miracles!

— *PT*

Q. There are many direct quotes from Jesus in the Gospels, as well as direct quotes from others. How can any of the writers quote what Jesus said to others decades before, when none of it was written in the newspapers or on TV, and most of them did not know Jesus? How accurate are the direct quotes in Scripture?

A. It's true that our modern Bible translations often employ quotation marks, which seem to imply a precise, direct quote. But such punctuation did not exist in the original Greek texts; it's a later addition. Also, consider that at the Last Supper Jesus told His apostles:

> "But the Counselor, the Holy Spirit, whom the Father will send in my name, he will teach you all things, and *bring to your remembrance all that I have said to you.*"

> — Jn 14:26, emphasis added

The sacred writers did not have to depend on their own unaided memories to recall accurately what Jesus and others had said decades before. God the Holy Spirit enabled them to do so.

In addition, the various Gospels sometimes provide slightly different wording when they are quoting the same statement of Our Lord or another person. (For example, certain statements of Jesus at the Last Supper are reported with small variations by Matthew, Mark, and Luke [see Mt 26:26-28; Mk 14:22-24; and Lk 22:17-20].) This variation suggests that, at times, the four

Evangelists were quoting indirectly rather than directly, expressing the sense of the statement without necessarily providing the precise wording.

In any case, even if some of these quotations are indirect rather than direct, that doesn't change the fact that they are reliable expressions of what was spoken by Jesus, His mother, and others. They tell the truth about what was said.

The Church's position, stated most recently in the Second Vatican Council's *Dogmatic Constitution on Divine Revelation*, is this:

> The divinely revealed realities, which are contained and presented in the text of sacred Scripture, have been written down under the inspiration of the Holy Spirit.

— N. 11

In other words, the canonical books of the Old and New Testaments "have God as their author, and have been handed on as such to the Church herself." God chose the authors, who used their "powers and faculties" to write exactly what God wanted written.

Therefore, the Church teaches that "the books of Scripture, firmly, faithfully and without error, teach that truth which God, for the sake of our salvation, wished to see confided to the sacred Scriptures."

— RR

Q. When did Jesus know that He was God?

A. At what point Our Lord's knowledge of himself as the divine Son of God incarnate was a full reality, we can only speculate. He was twelve years old at the time His parents "lost" Him and finally found Him in the temple (see Lk 2:41-51). His remark to them, "Why were you looking for me? Did you not know that I must be in my Father's house?" (v. 49), certainly suggests that by that time, He had already developed some awareness of His special identity.

Had Our Lady by this time revealed to Him the unique circumstances of His conception? Perhaps God the Father had directly revealed this knowledge to Him.

The matter has long been debated, with no definitive answer. St. Paul tells us that in becoming man, the Son of God "emptied Himself... coming in human likeness" (Phil 2:7). One aspect of that "emptying," it seems to me, was the limitation in knowledge He willingly took upon himself, for our sakes, in becoming fully human.

In that light, it's reasonable, I think, to assume that as an unborn child or infant He would not yet have had such knowledge, just as He apparently was limited to the physical capabilities of a normal child in those stages of development.

St. Luke tells us that the young Jesus "grew and became strong, filled with wisdom" and that He "increased in wisdom and in stature" (Lk 2:40, 52, RSV), which implies a mental as well as a physical development in His human nature as He matured.

It seems clear to me that by the time Jesus began His public ministry (at about the age of thirty), He knew fully who He was. The audible voice of God the Father coming out of heaven at His baptism, calling Him "My Son," would certainly have clarified the matter, if by any chance He still had any doubts at that point. (The reality was confirmed by the Father himself again at Our Lord's Transfiguration [see Lk 9:35].) And the devil's temptations in the wilderness immediately after Jesus' baptism took for granted that Jesus knew He was "the Son of God" with supernatural powers; it was part of Satan's strategy to challenge that conviction (see Lk 4:3, 9).

— *PT*

Q. When Lazarus died, Jesus knew he was going to rise again, so why did Our Lord weep?

A. Perhaps Our Lord was weeping, not so much for grief at losing His friend temporarily, but for grief over the universal predicament that had caused the death of Lazarus and of the whole human race: the rebellion of the human race He himself had created, with its terrible consequence, original sin. It may well be that those infinitely precious tears were shed for all of us, typified at that moment by Lazarus, who must suffer the pangs of bereavement and death.

If this is indeed the case, it should be comforting to know that Jesus was weeping for you and me, sharing our grief whenever we lose a loved one or must come face-to-face with our own mortality. It should remind us, too, that we can trust Our Lord to raise us all up on the last day.

— *PT*

Q. Did Jesus ever laugh?

A. Though the Gospels make no reference to Jesus laughing, I think it's safe to say that He did, in fact, laugh, and probably quite often. Here's why: the Church teaches us that Jesus Christ, though fully God, was fully human as well.

What could be more human than laughter? Could we possibly imagine a fully human Jesus living his entire human life on earth, including his childhood, without ever laughing?

Psychologists tell us that one of the common symptoms of certain kinds of psychosis is the inability to laugh. Laughter is a normal, healthy, natural aspect of the human condition; the inability to laugh is abnormal, pathological.

So why don't the Gospels ever mention that Jesus laughed? My guess is that they saw no need to mention it; they would have assumed that their readers didn't have to be told that He laughed just like everybody else.

At the same time, the four Evangelists do record occasions when it would have been quite natural for Our Lord to laugh. Some of His remarks have a sense of slapstick humor: for example, the blind leading the blind and falling into a ditch; Pharisees straining gnats and swallowing camels; the folly of hiding a lighted lamp under a bed, where it would ignite the sleeper — bed, pajamas, straw mattress, and all! (See Mt 23:24; Lk 6:39; 8:16.) I can imagine Jesus saying all these things with at least a twinkle in His eye, if not a chuckle.

Luke 10:21 tells us that on one particular occasion Jesus "rejoiced in the Holy Spirit." The Greek verb translated here as "rejoice" refers to exuberant celebration; it means, literally, "to jump for joy."

Is it so hard to imagine Jesus leaping for joy like a small child as He spoke specifically (as noted later in the same verse) about the importance of being childlike? And if He did that, is it so hard to imagine that He was laughing just as a small child would have laughed while He jumped?

G. K. Chesterton concludes his wonderful book Orthodoxy with the intriguing speculation that the Gospels say nothing of Jesus' laughter, not because He didn't laugh, but because He laughed only when He was alone: "There was some one thing that was too great for God to show us when He walked upon our earth," Chesterton suggests; "and I have sometimes fancied that it was His mirth."

— *PT*

Q. When Jesus forgave the adulterous woman, what was the punishment, if any, for the man with whom she committed adultery?

A. The Old Testament prescribes the same punishment — capital punishment — for both adulterers. "If a man commits adultery with the wife of his neighbor, both the adulterer and the adulteress shall be put to death" (Lev 20:10). "If a man is found lying with the wife of another man, both of them shall die, the man who lay with the woman, and the woman; so you shall purge the evil from Israel" (Deut 22:22).

Remember, now, that the scribes and Pharisees were enemies of Jesus, intent on trying to create some charge to bring against Him. Here they thought they had posed a dilemma for Him.

If He upheld the Old Testament law and agreed the adulteress should be executed, they would accuse Him of sedition; since A.D. 30, the Roman conquerors had forbidden Jews to carry out capital punishment. On the other hand, if Jesus said the woman should not be punished, they would accuse Him of breaking the Old Testament law.

So why didn't Jesus' enemies bring the guilty man along with the woman? That fact shows their motivation was not simply doing justice under the Jewish law. They were conspiring against Jesus. They evidently were using the woman in an attempt to trap Jesus in either sedition or heresy.

It is possible that they had sent someone (one of their own number?) to entice the woman into adultery and arranged to break in on the adulterous act. This, incidentally, would make them accessories to the crime of adultery and therefore guilty also. Perhaps this is what Jesus had in mind when He said, "Let him who is without sin among you be the first to throw a stone at her" (Jn 8:7).

— *RR*

Q. What is the significance of the 153 fish mentioned in the Gospel of John?

A. No one knows with certainty whether that number has a symbolic significance (see Jn 21:11). But we may be sure that Peter and the other professional fishermen would have counted their astonishing catch.

St. Jerome (c. 342-420), known as the "father of biblical studies," wrote that 153 species of fish had been identified by Greek zoologists. If that was true, or if — as others have suggested — there were 153 known countries at that time, we can see symbolic significance in the number.

Jesus had called the apostles to be "fishers of men" (Mt 4:19), and He had given them a commission to take the Gospel to the entire world (see Mt 28:18-20). The number, then, would symbolize the universal mission of the apostles (and under their leadership, the entire membership of the Church).

— *RR*

Q. **What do we know about Pilate's wife? The Gospel of Matthew tells us that she warned him not to harm Jesus. Do you think she might have been considering a conversion at that time?**

A. As you note, the Gospel says: "While he [Pilate] was still seated on the bench, his wife sent him a message, 'Have nothing to do with that righteous man. I suffered much in a dream today because of him' " (Mt 27:19).

We know nothing else of the governor's wife from Scripture — not even her name. But ancient traditions and legends sought to fill in some of the details.

The second-century theologian Origen, in his *Homilies on Matthew* (n. 35), suggests that Pilate's wife became a Christian, or at the very least that God sent her the dream mentioned by Matthew so that she would convert. Several other ancient and medieval writers took the same position, though others insisted that the dream was induced by the devil in an attempt to prevent Christ's saving death.

The apocryphal fourth-century text *Acts of Pilate* (also called the *Gospel of Nicodemus*) also mentions Pilate's wife, providing an elaborate version of the episode involving the dream. Various versions of the name that is commonly given to her, "Procula" ("Prokla," "Procle"), derive from this text, as do many of the subsequent legends surrounding both her and her husband. (Many centuries later, the name "Claudia" appears in some references to her as well.)

In some of the Eastern churches separated from Rome, Procula is venerated as a saint, whose feast day is October 27. In the Ethiopian Orthodox Church, both Procula and Pilate are venerated as saints whose joint feast day is June 25. This veneration would imply, of course, that both were eventually converted.

However, the ancient Church historian Eusebius reports otherwise. On the authority of earlier writers whom he does not name, he insists that Pilate fell into great misfortunes under the Roman emperor Caligula and eventually committed suicide (*Church History*, II.7).

— *PT*

Q. What and where was the "Decapolis"? The Gospels of Matthew and Mark refer to it.

A. *Decapolis*, which in Greek means "ten cities," is the name given in Scripture and by other ancient writers (such as Josephus, Ptolemy, Strabo, and Pliny) to a region in Palestine lying to the east and south of the Sea of Galilee. It took its name from a political alliance of the ten cities that dominated the area (though the area included other cities as well).

The Decapolis is referred to in the Gospels three times: Matthew 4:25, Mark 5:20, and Mark 7:31. Many Gentiles (non-Jews) lived in the region, including descendants of the veterans of the army of Alexander the Great, who had conquered the Middle East. Today the cities of the Decapolis, with the exception of Damascus, are deserted ruins.

— *PT*

Q. Were Jews ever swineherds? The ancient Jewish dietary laws forbid Jewish people to eat pork, but we read in the Gospels a couple of times about swineherds with their herds of pigs. Why would Jews have kept pigs if they couldn't eat pork?

A. You are correct that faithful Jews in Jesus' day could not eat pork because of the ancient dietary laws given by God, which declared pigs unclean (see Lev 11:1-8). But if you look closer at the Gospel passages referring to herds of swine, you find good reason to believe that they were owned not by Jews, but by Gentiles (people who were not Jews).

For example, when Jesus cast a "legion" of demons out of a man and into a herd of swine, He seems to have been in a locale on the far side of the Sea of Galilee, in an area where many Gentiles lived (see Mt 8:28-34; Mk 5:1-20; Lk 8:32-39). Ruins of an ancient town still stand on the traditional site of this exorcism, and the town was obviously built along Hellenistic (Greek) lines. It was part of the larger region widely known as an area with numerous Gentile residents.

— RR

Q. What's the difference between an apostle and a disciple?

A. *Disciple* is the more general term; it comes from the Greek word meaning "student" (related to our word *discipline*). So any faithful follower of Jesus could be designated a *disciple*, including people such as St. Mary Magdalene, St. Joseph of Arimathea, St. Nicodemus — and, indeed, even Our Lady.

The word *apostle* means, literally, "one sent out" or "missionary." The twelve *apostles* were chosen by Our Lord from among His many *disciples* and given a special mission and authority. Jesus sent them out "into all the world" to preach, teach, administer the sacraments, and govern the Church (see Mt 28:18-20).

> And when it was day, he called his disciples, and chose from them twelve, whom he named apostles; Simon, whom he named Peter, and Andrew his brother, and James and John, and Philip, and Bartholomew, and Matthew, and Thomas, and James the son of Alphaeus, and Simon who was called the Zealot, and Judas the son of James, and Judas Iscariot, who became a traitor.

> *— Lk 6:13*

(Notice that in this list and others, Peter is always named first, and Judas last, for obvious reasons.)

Whenever the Scripture speaks of the Twelve, it refers to these men. See, for example, John 6:66-71, which tells how some of Jesus' many disciples left him, but the Twelve remained with Him. Yet the word *apostle* is also applied in Scripture to other missionaries who were sent out to spread the Gospel, such as St. Paul and St. Barnabas. They were not among the Twelve, but they engaged in apostolic work.

— PT

Q. Were all the twelve apostles Jews?

A. We have no good reason from Scripture or Tradition to think otherwise. Some of the apostles (such as Phillip and Andrew) had Greek names, but this was not uncommon among Jewish people in the eastern Mediterranean region of that time, given that Hellenistic culture dominated that part of the world.

In addition, the apostles all worshipped in the Jewish Temple with Jesus (presumably in the inner courts where Gentiles weren't allowed), and they celebrated the Passover meal and other Jewish feasts with Him. So we can confidently assume, I think, that all were Jewish.

It's also important to note that the first Christians engaged in some internal debate over whether Gentiles (non-Jews) should be baptized and allowed to enter the Church (see Acts 10 and 11). If one of the Twelve whom Jesus chose as apostles had been a Gentile, it's hard to see how this issue would have arisen as a controversy in the early Church.

Finally, keep in mind that even if (as it seems) none of the twelve *apostles* was a Gentile, Jesus seems to have had other followers (disciples) who were not Jewish — presumably, people such as the Canaanite woman (Mt 15:21-28) and the Roman centurion (Mt 8:5-13).

— PT

Q. What day of the week was the Last Supper held on? All
    four Gospels agree that Jesus ate the Last Supper the day
    before He was crucified. But while Matthew, Mark, and
    Luke say the Last Supper was the Passover meal, John says
    that Jesus' trial (after the supper) was on "the day of Prep-
    aration for the Passover." What explanations have been
    offered to resolve this dilemma?

A. The apparent discrepancy you point out boils down to
this. The synoptic Gospels (Matthew, Mark, and Luke) tell us
Jesus celebrated the Passover before He was arrested and condemned. The fourth Gospel (John) informs us Jesus was crucified before the Passover began.

As we might expect, there are several theories to explain this
seeming discrepancy. Of these, the most convincing explanation
to me is one that seems to hold to the fourth Gospel's chronology
for the events of Holy Week. This theory reconciles the synoptic
and fourth Gospel accounts of Holy Week.

It starts with the now-known divisions among the Jews of
Jesus' time. There were quite a large number of "denominations"
among them, just as you find among Protestants today. They
were divided on many issues, especially with regard to the liturgical calendar.

The Sadducees and the priests who were in charge of the
Temple followed a lunar calendar of 354 days. That calendar set
the date of the Jewish festivals on the basis of lunar cycles. Thus,
Passover was celebrated on a different weekday (on the solar calendar) each year.

When the Dead Sea scrolls were discovered at Qumran, in
the middle of the last century, they revealed that the Essenes — a
Jewish sect of Jesus' time — had a different calendar. Theirs was
a 364-day solar calendar. On this calendar, the festivals always
occurred on the same day of the week.

The Jews who followed the Essene calendar always observed

the Passover on Tuesday night (which, for them, was the start of Wednesday). Did Jesus use the Essene calendar and celebrate the Passover with his disciples on Tuesday? Was the Last Supper, therefore, held on Tuesday night instead of Thursday night? Some scholars argue rather persuasively that this is indeed what happened.

In support of their argument, they point out that an Essene community did live inside the walls of Jerusalem, in the same part of the city where, according to tradition, the Upper Room was located. Jesus would have been aware that if He followed the Temple calendar, He would have died before He could celebrate the Passover. It is possible He decided to follow the Essene calendar and celebrate the Passover on Tuesday night.

This interpretation resolves two apparent chronological discrepancies between the Synoptics and the fourth Gospel. According to Mark 14:1, Christ's anointing at Bethany occurred "two days" before the Passover. Yet John 12:1 reports that event took place "six days" before the Passover. There would be no discrepancy if the Synoptics have in mind the Essene Passover on Tuesday; and the fourth Gospel, the Temple Passover on Friday evening.

After His arrest, but before His crucifixion, Jesus was subjected to lengthy legal procedures. He was brought before Annas (Jn 18:13, 19-23); before Caiaphas (Jn 18:24); before the Sanhedrin (Lk 22:66-71); before Herod (Lk 23:6-11); and before Pilate (Jn 18:28-40). All this could hardly have taken place in only a night and part of a day. The theory that Jesus celebrated the Passover on Tuesday night allows time for all these proceedings.

Three ancient sources agree in saying that Jesus presided at the Last Supper on a Tuesday night: a second- or third-century document called the *Didascalia Apostolorum*; St. Victorinus (third century); and St. Epiphanius (fourth century). The first two sources also tell us this is why early Christians fasted and did penance on Wednesdays and Fridays — these two days bracketed the time of the beginning and end of Jesus' passion.

Of one thing we are assured: the Gospels do not contradict one another.

> Holy Mother Church has firmly and with absolute constancy maintained and continues to maintain, that the four Gospels..., whose historicity she unhesitatingly affirms, faithfully hand on what Jesus, the Son of God, while He lived among men, really did and taught for their eternal salvation, until the day when he was taken up.
>
> — *Dogmatic Constitution on Divine Revelation*, N. 19

There is an explanation for the seeming discrepancy we have been discussing. We simply cannot at this point be certain what the explanation is; for now, we have only possible explanations.

— RR

Q. Was Jesus crucified through the wrists or the hands? I have heard that when Christ was nailed to the cross, the nails were actually driven through His wrists rather than His hands. Is this true?

A. In modern commentaries on the crucifixion, we read that the weight of Christ's precious Body would have torn the hands from the nails if they were pierced in the palms. So we assume that when Our Lord was crucified, the nails were driven through His wrists instead.

However, according to some researchers, the location of the piercing would most likely have been, not in what is popularly known today as the "wrist" (where wristwatches are worn), but rather in the "anatomical wrist," between the first and second row of carpal bones in the heel of the hand.

Jesus' reference to His wounded "hands" (Jn 20:27) is a matter of biblical translation. The Greek word translated here as "hand" (*cheir*) can actually refer to anything below the mid-forearm. For example, Acts 12:7 uses this same Greek word to tell how the chains fell from St. Peter's "hands," even though the chains would presumably have been placed around what we would call the "wrists."

— RR

Q. Why did the soldiers break the legs of the two men crucified with Jesus?

A. According to those who have studied the grim mechanics of crucifixion, in order to breathe adequately, the crucified victim periodically had to push himself up using his legs. Breaking the legs prevented him from doing that, thus hastening his death. He would suffocate.

The people asked Pilate to break the legs of Jesus and the two thieves crucified with Him so that they would die quickly, allowing their bodies to be taken down from the crosses before the Sabbath (which began at sunset). They broke the legs of the thieves but not of Jesus because they discovered that He was already dead. But just to make sure, one soldier (according to tradition, named Longinus) thrust his lance into Jesus' side (Jn 19:33-34).

As it turns out, that scenario fulfilled Messianic prophecies (as John pointed out): "Not a bone of it will be broken" and "They will look upon Him whom they have pierced" (Jn 19:36-37; see also Ex 12:46; Num 9:12; Ps 34:20; Zech 12:10).

— PT

Q. The Gospel of Luke and the Acts of the Apostles are actually two parts of the same work. Why are Luke and Acts separated if they were written by the same person?

A. St. Luke wrote both these books, apparently — according to Acts 1:1 — as two volumes of the same work (the Greek word translated there as "book" is *logos*, and can be rendered in English as either "book" or "volume"). The Gospel ends at the point where Acts begins: with the ascension of Our Lord into heaven (see Lk 24:50-53; Acts 1:1-2). So, in a way, it would make sense to arrange the New Testament books with Acts immediately following Luke.

Nevertheless, a different criterion for arranging the books is employed here.

From the beginning, the Gospels have been considered by the Church as the most important of the New Testament books, first in honor, and "the heart of all the Scriptures, 'because they are our principal source for the life and teaching of the Incarnate Word, our Savior' " (*CCC* 125, citing the *Dogmatic Constitution on the Divine Revelation* [*Dei Verbum*], N. 18).

Not surprisingly, the New Testament ordering reflects this primacy of the Gospels, placing them all together and before all the other books. So the Book of Acts could not be placed among the four Gospels in order to keep it next to Luke, with an arrangement such as Matthew, Mark, Luke, Acts, and John.

Why not simply place Luke as the last of the four Gospels, then, so that Acts comes immediately after it? The ordering of the Gospels does vary in the ancient lists that have survived, and some of those lists have placed Luke at the last, probably for that very reason.

Nevertheless, the order that seems to have been the most ancient, which St. Jerome used in the Vulgate (his fourth-century translation of the Bible into Latin), was Matthew, Mark, Luke, John. This order became the standard, most likely because it reflects the chronological order of the Gospels' composition according to ancient tradition. That tradition suggests that Matthew was composed first and John last, with Mark and Luke in between. Given this order, Luke and Acts had to be separated.

— *PT*

Q. What's the meaning of the number 666 in Scripture?

A. In Revelation 13, we read about St. John's vision of the two beasts who, for a time, will exert their power in the world.

Verses 17 and 18 give a hint for identifying the second beast. Its name is encoded in a number, 666. (Some ancient manuscripts read "616" instead of "666," and some recent historical evidence suggests that "616" is, in fact, the more likely original reading.)

The "real meaning" of this number is unclear and has been widely debated for many centuries. As you'll find in the footnotes on this passage in several versions of the Bible, each letter of the alphabets used in ancient Greek and Hebrew (the two primary languages of biblical texts) has a numerical value as well. A number of letter combinations in various names can thus add up to 666 or 616, and a number of historical figures have been "nominated" for this dubious honor.

One likely possibility is the Roman emperor Caesar Nero. The Greek form of his name in Hebrew letters yields the sum of 666, and the Latin form yields 616. When the book was written, Nero was known to Christians as a vicious enemy of the Church, responsible for countless martyrdoms — so it would certainly be fitting to view him as the "beast" depicted in this passage.

— PT

Q. Is it true that some anti-Catholics have claimed the pope is the "beast" in Revelation?

It is true. Since the time of the Protestant Reformation, some anti-Catholic apologists have claimed that Revelation 13:18 refers to the pope as the enemy of the true faith. His title, they say, is *Vicarius Filii Dei* (Vicar of the Son of God). Using the value of Roman numerals, the sum of the letters in that title is 666.

Here's how the calculation works. As in Greek and Hebrew, some Latin letters are used for numbers. "I" = 1; "V" = 5; "X" = 10; "L" = 50; "C" = 100; ""D" = 500; "M" = 1,000. Letters that have no numerical value are to be ignored in calculating the numerical significance of a name. The letter "U" is treated as "V." Since there is no "W" in Latin, it is rendered as "VV."

The Latin title *Vicarius Filii Dei*, then, would be VICARIVS

FILII DEI. Now apply this numbering scheme to it. You get these numbers: 5 (V) + 1 (I) + 100 (C) + 1 (I) + 5 (V) + 1 (I) + 50 (L) + 1 (I); + 1 (I) + 500 (D) + 1 (I). The total is 666. Therefore, according to these anti-Catholic apologists, Scripture plainly identifies the pope as one of the two beasts who tried to destroy the true faith.

To unwind all this, start with the fact that *Vicarius Filii Dei* is *not* the pope's title. It is never used in any official Church document. His title is "Vicar of Christ" (*Vicarius Christi*), which — according to the scheme given above — adds up to 214. The Pope has other titles: *Servus Servorum Dei* (Servant of the Servants of God), *Pontifex Maximus* (Supreme Pontiff), and *Successor Petri* (Successor of Peter). None comes even close to adding up to 666.

Incidentally, this false identification of the beast in Revelation 13:18 with the pope has often been made in Seventh-day Adventist literature. Ironically enough, if we were to apply this numbering scheme to the name of the founder of the Adventists, Ellen Gould White, her name in Latin adds up to 666. According to Adventist logic, then, must we conclude that the founder of their denomination is "the beast"?

Cardinal John Henry Newman commented on the polemical attempts to equate the pope or the Catholic Church with one of the beasts or with the Antichrist. He saw in those attempts a dim, distorted perception of the truth about the Church. These opponents of the Church, he said, looking at her from the outside, recognize that she is no ordinary institution, that she is indeed supernatural. Since she cannot be of Christ, they reason, she must be of Satan. That slander, in other words, at least acknowledges part of the truth about her — that she is the supernatural Mystical Body of Christ.

— *RR*

Q. Does the Bible forbid drinking alcohol?

A. The Bible warns against the *abuse* of alcohol, especially in the book of Proverbs: "Wine is a mocker, strong drink a brawler;

and whoever is led astray by it is not wise" (Prov 20:1, RSV). "Be not among winebibbers [that is, those who drink to excess]" (Prov 23:20, RSV). This latter passage goes on to describe vividly the evil effects — both physical and psychological — of drunkenness (vv. 29-35).

In the New Testament, St. Paul forbids "drinking bouts" (Gal 5:21) and insists: "Do not get drunk on wine, in which lies debauchery" (Eph 5:18).

Nevertheless, Scripture doesn't forbid drinking alcohol altogether; it allows for moderate consumption. Jesus turned water into wine at the wedding party in Cana so the wedding guests could enjoy it (Jn 2:1-11). St. Paul instructed St. Timothy, "Stop drinking only water, but have a little wine for the sake of your stomach and your frequent illnesses" (1 Tim 5:23).

Use a biblical concordance to look up all the occurrences of the word "wine" in Scripture and you'll find that the great majority of them take a neutral or even positive attitude toward it. (Wine is the most commonly mentioned alcoholic beverage in the Bible, though there are also a few references to "strong drink," such as Proverbs 31:6).

Wine, the Bible says, is a sign of divine blessing (Deut 3:28). It was part of the tithe to Old Testament priests and the libations at the altar (Deut 18:4; Ex 29:40). The psalmist rejoiced that God "brings[s] bread from the earth, and wine to gladden our hearts" (Ps 104:14-15).

— *PT*

Q. Does the Bible say that you cannot get any type of tattoo?

A. Comments about the Bible forbidding tattoos and piercings probably refer to laws in the Old Testament book of Leviticus. Leviticus 19:28 says: "You shall not make any cuttings in your flesh or tattoo any marks upon you." A similar law is given in Deuteronomy 14:1, which says: "You shall not cut yourselves or make any baldness on your foreheads for the dead."

Some of the laws given in these Old Testament books had
to do with eternal moral principles, such as laws in Leviticus forbidding idolatry (Lev 19:4); stealing and lying (Lev 19:11); and,
in the previous chapter, forbidding homosexual acts and bestial-
ity (Lev 18:22-23). Other laws, however, were dependent on the
culture of the time because their primary intent was to keep the
Israelites separated from pagan cultures, which often included
horrendous customs (such as sacrificing a firstborn to a god by
burning the infant alive [see Lev 20:2]).

The two laws about tattooing and body mutilation probably
fall in the second category. The words from Deuteronomy and
other passages suggest that these practices were forbidden to the
ancient Israelites because they were a part of the pagan religious
customs of the peoples they encountered. The Hebrews needed to
avoid such practices in order to maintain purity in their worship
of the one true God.

Though someone today could perhaps make a case against
these practices for other reasons (even religious reasons), it would
be problematic to use these particular verses to support the idea
that God forbids people today to get tattoos or piercings — just
as you wouldn't claim that the law in the same biblical chapter against trimming beards (Lev 19:27) would apply today. The
same goes for the Old Testament dietary laws forbidding the
ancient Israelites to eat pork or shellfish.

For Christians, the biblical laws separating believers in God
from non-believers, given to the ancient Israelites, no longer apply
except in cases where an eternal moral, theological, or spiritual
principle is involved.

For more about this issue, read Acts 10:1-48; 15:1-35.

— *PT*

Q. **Does the Bible forbid foul language?**

A. It does, indeed.

Some specific instructions in Scripture:

Let not your mouth become used to coarse talk, for in it lies sinful matter.

— Sir 23:13, NAB

When a godless man curses his adversary, he really curses himself.

— Sir 21:27, NAB

Immorality or any impurity or greed must not even be mentioned among you, as is fitting among holy ones, no obscenity or silly or suggestive talk, which is out of place.

— Eph 5:3-4, NAB

Bless those who persecute you; bless and do not curse them.

— Rom 12:14

Put to death, then, the parts of you that are earthly: immorality, impurity, passion, evil desire, and the greed that is idolatry. Because of these the wrath of God is coming [upon the disobedient].... [Y]ou must put them all away: anger, fury, malice, slander, and obscene language out of your mouths.

— Col 3:5-8, NAB

Avoid profane, idle talk, for such people will become more and more godless.

— 2 Tim 2:16, NAB

No foul language should come out of your mouths, but only such as is good for needed edification, that it may impart grace to those who hear.

— Eph 4:20, NAB

When we say "foul language," we should note first that we're referring to a whole range of speech: *vulgarity* (crude or coarse language, usually having to do with body parts or functions); *obscenity* (language that's lewd or otherwise contrary to sexual purity); *profanity* (words with sacred or theological meanings used in a flippant or perverse way, such as "God," "Jesus," "Christ," "damn," or "hell"). Two subsets of profanity would be *cursing* (expressing a desire that someone suffer ill, especially damnation) and *blasphemy* (the abuse or careless use of God's name).

The misuse of God's name is an extremely serious sin. Remember the second commandment:

> "You shall not take the name of the Lord your God in vain. For the Lord will not leave unpunished him who takes His name in vain."

> — Ex 20:7

In Old Testament times, blasphemers were actually stoned to death.

> — *PT*

Q. Why should we be concerned about our language? Isn't it "just words"?

A. Let's take a look at what Scripture says:

- *They may be "just words," but they have remarkable power to impact people for good or evil.*

  Death and life are in the power of the tongue.

  > — Prov 18:21

- *Our words are an indicator of what's in our mind and heart.* Jesus said:

  "For from the fullness of the heart the mouth speaks.

A good person brings forth good out of a store of goodness, but an evil person brings forth evil out of a store
of evil."

— Mt 12:34-36, NAB

• *We'll be judged by God for the words we use in this life.*
Our Lord's solemn warning:

"I tell you, on the day of judgment people will render
an account for every careless word they speak. By your
words you will be acquitted, and by your words you
will be condemned."

— Mt 12:36-37

See also James 3:1-12 about the power of the tongue.

— *PT*

**Q. What is the "unforgivable sin," "blasphemy against the
Holy Spirit"?**

A. In three parallel passages in the Gospels, Jesus speaks of
sin against the Holy Spirit: Matthew 12:31-32, Mark 3:28-29,
and Luke 12:10. St. Luke's version is the most succinct: "Everyone who speaks a word against the Son of Man will be forgiven;
but the one who blasphemes against the Holy Spirit will not be
forgiven."

The first clause of this sentence reminds us that a person who
is mistaken about Jesus, who does not know Jesus as the Son of
God, can be forgiven for not acknowledging Him.

To understand the second clause, we must first note a
basic truth: God limits himself with regard to human freedom.
Although He always includes in His overall plan even our misuse
of our freedom, He always respects that freedom and will not
destroy it.

He therefore does not force himself on us, so to speak — does not force us to accept His love and forgiveness. Our freedom gives us the frightful capacity to reject Him and to refuse to allow Him to forgive us.

The "unforgivable sin" is the sin of refusing to be forgiven. It is the determination to continue in sin at all costs.

In his encyclical *Dominum et Vivificantem* (*Lord and Giver of Life*, 1986), Pope John Paul II taught:

> If Jesus says that blasphemy against the Holy Spirit cannot be forgiven either in this life or in the next, it is because this "non-forgiveness" is linked, as to its cause, to "non-repentance," in other words to the radical refusal to be converted.

> — N. 46

Sometimes sincere Christians ask themselves whether, in fact, they have committed the unforgivable sin. If one asks that question in awe and even in fear, the very asking shows that a person has not committed the unforgivable sin.

— RR

2.

Questions about Church Teaching

Q. What was God doing before He created the universe?

A. Did you know that people were asking this same question at least sixteen centuries ago? In his *Confessions*, St. Augustine of Hippo (354-430) notes that he had been challenged to answer it. His answer was rather impish: before He created the universe, Augustine said, perhaps God was busy creating hell for people who are too curious about such matters!

Of course, he was joking — just one more piece of evidence that the saints have a fine sense of humor. But the truth is that we can't truly speak of a "time" before the creation of the universe because that act of the Almighty included the creation of time itself.

Nevertheless, we can say that even in the absence of a created universe, God would have been doing what it is His nature to do: to love and enjoy. "God is love," 1 John 4:8 tells us, and joy is the fruit of love.

Without creatures to love, you might ask, what would have been the object of God's love? Within the Triune Godhead, from before all eternity, the Father has loved the Son, and the Son has loved the Father, with a Love that is, in fact, a divine Person himself: the Holy Spirit. Just think of the abyss of joy flowing within that infinite Trinity!

— PT

Q. Why did God allow Adam and Eve to eat of the fruit of the tree of the knowledge of good and evil? He knew they would be tempted, so why did He let this first sin happen?

A. Another way to state your question is this: *Why did God make human beings with free will even though He knew they would abuse it?*

Which is better — a world of robots who act only in accordance with God's will because they are programmed to do so, or a world of sons and daughters who are free to love Him and one another even if they sometimes fail to do so? I think that most of us would agree with God's decision that the latter is the better kind of world, despite its problems.

As long as there exists in the world a free will other than God's own, there exists the possibility of that will opposing His will, at least at the outset. (A human free will that chooses to love God is at last, after death, confirmed in that choice so that it can never choose against God again; but the final "ratification" of the will's choice by God results from the will's own free choice in the first place.)

God was willing to take the risk that free human (and angelic) wills would oppose Him because free-willed creatures are a much higher good than robots. But keep in mind as well that God is able to bring out of even the greatest of evils a greater good.

Because He has this ability (which He continually exercises), He is justified in allowing the evil. In the end, though we may not be able to see it clearly now, His Providence crafts a universe in which, as St. Paul says, "this slight momentary affliction is preparing for us an eternal weight of glory beyond all comparison" (2 Cor 4:17).

— *PT*

Q. If we're made in God's image, why are we born into the world as sinners?

A. We are truly made in God's image (see Gen 1:26-27). That means we are, like God himself, persons: we have a rational intellect that can think, and we have a free will that can love and make other choices.

Nevertheless, the image of God in us has been marred, like the image of a face on a coin that has become scratched and worn. Our intellects have been darkened and our wills have been bent in the wrong directions.

How did this happen?

Because of what we call original sin.

Our first human parents used their free wills to turn against God through sin. The result was that they lost the righteousness they originally possessed. They could not pass on to their offspring what they themselves no longer possessed, so all their descendants (except for Jesus and His mother) have been born with a deficiency, a defect, that we call original sin.

This defect deforms God's image in us, but it cannot totally erase that image. We still have the ability to think and love and choose. Yet the deformity is compounded by our actual sins — the wrong choices we make.

We can be grateful that the sacrament of Baptism washes away original sin in us. Nevertheless, we are still left with a weakness called concupiscence, the tendency to sin.

How does concupiscence work? It doesn't force us to sin. Rather, it inclines us to do so. It's as if we walk on an incline that leaves us sliding down into sin if we don't actively resist the slide.

We can rejoice that God's image is not totally obliterated even in the most wicked human being. That means we can hope for a person's salvation no matter how hopeless a cause he or she may seem. It also means that no matter how terrible we know our own sins to be, we can hope for God's grace to save us, too.

— PT

Q. Can we repent of original sin?

A. Original sin is a deficiency of sanctifying grace and supernatural life in the damaged human nature we have inherited from our first parents, as a result of their sin. Actual sin, on the other hand, is sin that we have personally committed by an act of our own free will.

For this reason, we can repent of actual sins, having genuine sorrow for what we have done or failed to do, and intending to do better. But we can't "repent" of original sin in that way, since it comes to us apart from our free will and is not of our own doing.

Nevertheless, this doesn't mean we can't do anything about original sin. The sacrament of Baptism cleanses us both of original sin and of actual sins committed up to the time we're baptized. That's why it's so important for Catholic parents to have their children baptized as soon after birth as possible. And if an adult has not been baptized and still carries original sin, he or she can "repent" of the failure to do so, and then seek entrance into the Church through Baptism.

— *PT*

Q. What is the nature of the soul according to Catholic teaching? What is the nature of the connection (if any) between the body and soul? Specifically, why do the actions of our body affect the fate of our soul?

A. The *Catechism of the Catholic Church* points out that Sacred Scripture often uses the word "soul" to denote a human life, or the totality of a human person:

But "soul" also refers to the innermost aspect of man, that which is of greatest value in him, that by which he is most especially in God's image: "soul" signifies the *spiritual principle* in man.

— *CCC* 363

That is, the soul is what animates the body; it is the seat, so to speak, of human personality. The soul is the seat of our intellect and our will, including such aspects as consciousness, reason, memory, imagination, emotion, and conscience.

In this life, soul and body are joined in intimate union. For that reason, whatever affects the soul affects the body, and vice versa. This union is so close that the body and soul aren't separate natures within us; together, they form a single human nature.

Because of the close union between body and soul, the actions of the body necessarily affect the condition and the fate of the soul. We're not morally responsible for the actions of purely bodily functions. But every time in the body we freely perform an immoral action, it is only because our soul — the animating principle — has chosen that action.

This is why conscious bodily actions have eternal consequences. This is why Sacred Scripture tells us that "we must all appear before the judgment seat of Christ, so that each one may receive good or evil, according to *what he has done in the body*" (2 Cor 5:10, emphasis added).

God has created the soul to be everlasting, but the body is mortal. When a human being dies, body and soul separate. The body is the portion of human nature that has been left behind; the soul is the portion that has departed.

Nevertheless, just as Jesus' soul was raised in His resurrection body, so will our souls be embodied in glorified bodies, if we die in Christ.

— *RR*

Q. Does Jesus have a soul?

A. Your question was raised in the early centuries of the Church as Christians were trying to more accurately discern the nature of the Incarnation. In time, the Church gave a definitive answer: when God the Son became a man, He took for himself a complete human nature. That is to say, the human nature He took (the technical theological term is "assumed") included everything that makes us human.

Human beings have a single nature, composed of both a body and a spirit. In humans, this spirit also functions as the soul, which is defined as the animating principle of a body — that is, the thing that gives life to the body. (Note that body and soul are not two natures, but two components so intimately joined that they form together a single human nature.)

Consequently, when God the Son became a man, He took for himself not only a human body, but also a human soul. This means that the Incarnate God had (and will always have — He will never lose them) two natures: one divine, and one human, with the human nature being composed of both body and soul.

Why was it so important for the Church to clarify this reality? Because, as the Church Fathers often emphasized, the purpose of the Incarnation was to heal and save human nature; so, if some part of that nature was not included in the Incarnation, it would not have been saved and healed, either.

Do we fallen human beings need healing in our souls? Of course! Jesus came to heal the disorder of our souls: our thinking, our will, our emotions. So He took a human soul as well as a body; that's why, for example, we see Him weeping over the death of His friend Lazarus (see Jn 11:35).

This reality is also reflected in the traditional formulation that when we receive Our Lord in the Eucharist, we are receiving not only His Body and Blood, but also His "Soul and Divinity." His Body and Soul are so intimately joined, and His Humanity and Divinity so completely in union, that to receive any one of these is to receive them all — the whole Person, Jesus Christ, the Son of God in the flesh.

— *PT*

Q. Jesus is both fully God and fully human. Isn't being sinful part of our fallen human nature? If so, how can we say that Jesus was "fully human" if He never sinned?

A. When our first parents fell from grace, they damaged the human nature that God had created for them. It became disordered, twisted, broken. Consequently, they could not pass on to their descendants what they themselves no longer possessed. The original sin that now affects all of us is thus a deficiency in human nature, a lack of the original righteousness with which the human race was created.

In this light, then, we come to see that it is precisely Jesus' sinlessness that makes Him fully human. In His perfect, unfallen human nature, He is the kind of man that God originally intended. Nothing is lacking in His human nature, nothing damaged or diminished by sin.

On the other hand, because we are sinners, we are actually — to one extent or another — less than fully human. You and I have not, in this life, attained to the full human perfection for which God has created us.

God willing, we will one day reach that full perfection of humanity when we stand before Him in heaven, enjoying the Beatific Vision. Then we, too, will be "fully human"!

— PT

Q. Did Jesus come to earth to die?

A. Yes. Jesus repeatedly declared that He had come not to do His own will, but the will of His Father as God's means of redeeming a fallen, sinful world. Four different times He told His disciples that He would be put to death (see Mt 17:22-23 [and parallels in Mk 9:30-32 and Lk 9:43-45]; Mt 16:21; 20:12-19; 26:2).

On four occasions, Jesus spoke of His imminent passion and death as a "cup" that His Father had given Him to drink. In the Garden of Gethsemane, Jesus prayed three times, "My Father, if it is possible, let this cup pass from me; nevertheless, not as I will, but as thou wilt" (Mt 26:39, 42, 44). When the crowd came to arrest Jesus, Peter started to resist with his sword. Jesus stopped him, asking rhetorically, "Shall I not drink the cup which the Father has given me?" (Jn 18:11).

Actually, to show that Jesus came to die, you need quote only one brief Gospel text. Speaking of His mission, Jesus said, "The Son of Man did not come to be served but to serve and *to give His life* as a ransom for many" (Mt 20:28, emphasis added).

— *RR*

Q. Why does Jesus' bodily resurrection matter? Isn't it His message that counts?

A. St. Paul put it most bluntly:

If Christ has not been raised, then our preaching is in vain and your faith is in vain. We are even found to be misrepresenting God, because we testified of God that he raised Christ, whom he did not raise if it is true that the dead are not raised.

— 1 Cor 15:14-15

The resurrection of Jesus isn't separate from His message; it's an essential aspect of that message, of one piece with the rest of the Gospel. Deny it, and we might as well deny all the rest as an unreliable fabrication. Christ's rising from the dead is integral to the testimony of the Church about who Jesus is, what He said, and what He did, a seal of authenticity on everything else.

The *Catechism* puts it this way:

The Resurrection above all constitutes the confirmation of all Christ's works and teachings. All truths, even those most inaccessible to human reason, find their justification if Christ by his Resurrection has given the definitive proof of his divine authority, which he had promised.

Christ's Resurrection is the fulfillment of the promises both of the Old Testament and of Jesus himself during his earthly life.... The truth of Jesus' divinity is confirmed by his Resurrection.

— *CCC* 651-53

At the same time, Christ's resurrection is the source of our present life with God, which came about after the death of our old life trapped in sin.

> The Paschal mystery has two aspects: by his death, Christ, liberates us from sin; by his Resurrection, he opens for us the way to a new life ... and a new participation in grace.

> — *CCC* 654

Finally, Christ's resurrection is essential to Christian faith because, as St. Paul went on to say, without it "those who have fallen asleep in Christ have perished" (1 Cor 15:18). Our own hope of resurrection is based on the reality of His.

> Christ, "the first-born from the dead" (*Col* 1:18), is the principle of our own resurrection, even now by the justification of our souls (cf. *Rom* 6:4), and one day by the new life He will impart to our bodies (cf. *Rom* 8:11).

> — *CCC* 658

> — *PT*

Q. Was Jesus' resurrection essentially the same as the raising of Lazarus from the dead?

A. Not at all. As the *Catechism* states:

> Christ's Resurrection was not a return to earthly life, as was the case with the raisings from the dead that he had performed before Easter: Jairus' daughter, the young man of Naim, Lazarus. These actions were miraculous events, but the persons miraculously raised were returned by Jesus' power to ordinary earthly life. At some particular moment they would die again. Christ's Resurrection is essentially different. In his risen body he passes from the state of death to another life beyond time and space. At Jesus'

Resurrection his body is filled with the power of the Holy
Spirit: he shares the divine life in his glorious state.

— *CCC* 646

Indications of this transformation are clear in the Gospel
accounts. Christ's resurrected body now has new capabilities: He
can appear and reappear suddenly; He can pass through locked
doors; He can conceal His identity even from those who know
Him well (see Lk 24:13-37; Jn 20:11-19). Then, at the appointed
time of His last appearance, He is able to ascend into heaven
in this transformed body (see Lk 24:50-51), bringing about "the
irreversible entry of his humanity into divine glory" (*CCC* 659).

— *PT*

**Q. How could the same Spirit who was sent by the Father and
the Son after Jesus' ascension into heaven have already
been at work in the world since its creation?**

A. God is present in His world in different ways and at different "levels," we might say. Scripture tells us that the Holy Spirit,
who is God, was active in the creation of the world (see Gen 1:2).
He has remained present in the world as the One who renews His
creation (Ps 104:30) and who inspires human creativity (Ex 31:3;
35:31) and other gifts (Judg 3:10; 6:34).

On certain occasions throughout history, God the Holy
Spirit has been present in what we might call a more "focused"
way, when He has prompted people to speak on His behalf (for
example, 2 Sam 23:2), most especially the prophets (see Is 61:1-
3). On these occasions, Scripture speaks of His "coming upon"
someone or "filling" someone.

God the Holy Spirit was present in a unique way at the incarnation of God the Son. In a mystery we don't fully understand,
the Spirit came upon Mary so that she conceived Jesus "by the
power of the Holy Spirit," and in time gave birth to a Son who
was both God and man. The same Spirit spoke through St. Eliza-

beth (Lk 1:41-45) and St. Zachariah (vv. 67-79), and prompted St. Simeon to come to the temple to meet the Holy Family (2:27).

Years later, the Spirit "descended upon [Jesus] in bodily form like a dove" (3:21) at His baptism, so that Jesus was "filled with the Holy Spirit" (4:1). This doesn't mean that before His baptism, Jesus did not have the Holy Spirit present with Him. It simply refers to a different kind of presence — one more intense, focused, "concentrated," so to speak, and more clearly discernible to others.

In the same way, when Jesus promised to ask God the Father to send the Spirit to His followers, He wasn't saying that their lives up until that time were void of the Spirit. Instead, He was saying that the Spirit would be present to them and in them, would inspire them and work through them — we might say, would *possess* them — in a new way. They would be *clothed* with the Spirit, filled with the Spirit, *baptized* (that is, *immersed*) in the Spirit (Lk 3:16, 24:49; Jn 14:16-17; Acts 1:5, 2:4). The initial fulfillment of this promise, of course, took place on the Day of Pentecost (see Acts 2).

Here's an admittedly imperfect analogy: human persons, who are made in the image of the three divine Persons (Father, Son, and Holy Spirit), can similarly be "present" to others in various ways.

For example, I can be "present" to my wife at different levels. I can be present physically, so that she's able to touch me. I can be present in a different way through a phone call, so that even though I'm physically distant, she can hear my voice. I can be present through a letter or e-mail, so that she knows my thoughts. And even if I haven't contacted her in these ways, I can be present in her memory, so that she recalls my appearance, voice, past actions, and thoughts. Finally, if death should separate us, I hope to die in friendship with God, so that I can be present to my wife in a whole new and marvelous way through the communion of saints.

— PT

Q. What does it mean to say the Holy Spirit "proceeds" from the Father and the Son?

A. This is a technical theological term to describe the relation of the divine Persons within the very nature God himself. Entire books have been written about this mystery, but one way to summarize it is to say that the eternal love between the Father and the Son is so real, so substantial, that this love is itself a third divine Person who "proceeds" or "comes forth" from them — the Holy Spirit.

— PT

Q. What is the meaning of the theological term *theosis*?

A. The biblically-rooted Catholic teaching about the nature of the salvation offered us in Christ is known as the doctrine of *theosis* or *theopoiesis*. It has been preached since the early centuries of the Church and is prominent in the Eastern churches as well. The Greek terms are often translated in English with the startling words "divinization" or "deification."

The reality described by *theosis* is affirmed at every Mass in the words of the priest: "Through the mystery of this water and wine may we come to share in the divinity of Christ, who humbled himself to share in our humanity."

What do these words mean?

The Scripture tells us that God has made certain "precious and very great promises" through which we will "come to *have a share in the divine nature*" (2 Pet 1:3, 4, emphasis added). This is possible because in Christ, the nature of God himself has been joined to the nature of humanity, and the resulting redeemed human nature, which is "in Christ," now has new possibilities. As the ancient theologians put it: *What God is by nature, we can become by grace.*

What exactly are those "precious promises" that reveal what it means to have a share in God's own nature? Look at certain divine attributes, and you'll find that in Scripture the saints have been promised these attributes as a part of their ultimate perfection in Christ:

Divine knowledge.

> For our knowledge is imperfect and our prophecy is imperfect . . . For now we see in a mirror dimly, but then face to face. Now I know in part; then I shall understand fully, as I am fully understood.
>
> — 1 Cor 13:9, 12

Divine glory.

> We are children of God, and if children, then heirs, heirs of God and fellow heirs with Christ, provided we suffer with him in order that we may also be glorified with him.
>
> — Rom 8:16-17

> And we all, with unveiled face, beholding the glory of the Lord, are being changed into his likeness from one degree of glory to another.
>
> — 2 Cor 3:18

> So I exhort the elders among you, as . . . a partaker in the glory that is to be revealed.
>
> — 1 Pet 5:1

Divine authority and power.

> If we endure, we shall also reign with him.
>
> — 2 Tim 2:12

> The Lord God shall be their light, and they shall reign for ever and ever.
>
> — Rev 22:5

"He who conquers and who keeps my works until the end, I will give power over the nations ... as I myself have received power from my Father."

— Rev 2:26-27

Divine holiness.

He disciplines us for our good, that we may share his holiness. ... Strive for peace with all men, and for the holiness without which no one will see the Lord.

— Heb 12:10, 14

"You, therefore, must be perfect, as your heavenly Father is perfect."

— Mt 5:48

You have come to ... the spirits of just men made perfect.

— Heb 12:22-23

Divine love.

If we love one another, God abides in us and his love is perfected in us.

— 1 Jn 4:12

Divine life.

God gave us eternal life, and this life is in His Son. . . . we are in him who is true, in his Son Jesus Christ. This is the true God and eternal life.

— 1 Jn 5:11, 20

In short, says St. Paul, we are to be "filled with all the fullness of God" (Eph 3:19). Or, as St. John sums it up for us:

> Beloved, we are God's children now; it does not yet appear what we shall be, but we know that when he appears we shall be like him, for we shall see him as he is.

— 1 Jn 3:2

This destiny of the saints is, of course, what is traditionally called the *Beatific Vision*, the vision of perfect blessedness. When we are finally perfected in heaven, we will at last see God face-to-face, and we will be like the One we behold — because we will have a share in His divine nature.

— *PT*

Q. Does the level of our spiritual maturity at the moment of death determine where we will spend eternity? This notion implies different levels of heavenly attainment for souls after purgatory, rather that the attainment of perfection in the "Beatific Vision" of those who obtain heaven.

A. To say that the redeemed will attain perfection is not the same as saying that they will attain equality. For those of us who, before entering heaven, must first enter the intermediate state of purgatory, it will be a process of purifying the love for God that, by His grace, we have attained in this life.

In other words, the depth of the love we have at the moment of death is the depth at which we shall be glorified. The level of spiritual maturity we have attained by grace at the moment of death is the level at which we shall be perfected through our life in purgatory, the level at which we shall spend eternity. Our love for God, and for those around us, will be perfected but not increased.

Consider this analogy. Beside a fifty-gallon drum place a

thimble. Fill them both with water. Now, one is just as full as the other, but the capacity is greatly different.

This image illustrates what the Church teaches: in the lives of the redeemed in heaven there will be varying "degrees of blessedness." Different persons will have different capacities for union with God, based on the sanctity each has achieved by grace in this life. All of us will be filled to perfection, though not all of us to the same capacity.

Nevertheless, there will, of course, be no envy in heaven. Those of us who will be like thimbles will forever rejoice in the saints who will be like tank trucks.

Jesus assured us, "In my Father's house are many rooms" (Jn 14:2). St. Augustine taught that the reference to "rooms" or "mansions" refers to differing degrees of rewards in heaven, and St. Thomas Aquinas concurred.

In 1439, the Council of Florence taught that those who have incurred no sin after baptism, as well as those who have been cleansed of all stain from sin, will "clearly behold the triune God as He is, *yet one person more perfectly than another according to the difference of their merits*" (emphasis added). The Greek version of that conciliar teaching ends with the words "according to the worth of their lives."

The Second Vatican Council's *Dogmatic Constitution on the Church* says this of the life of the redeemed in heaven:

> All of us, however, *in varying degrees* and in different ways, share in the same charity towards God and our neighbors, and we all sing the one hymn of glory to our God.
>
> — N. 49, emphasis added

In 1979, the Congregation for the Doctrine of the Faith issued a "Letter on Eschatology." It stated clearly that "*our charity on earth will be the measure of our sharing in God's glory in heaven*" (emphasis in the original).

True love always desires the deepest possible union appropriate to the relationship with the beloved. If we truly love God, our Father, Jesus, our Savior, and the Holy Spirit, our life-giver, we want to share in their life to the fullest possible extent. Thus, you can see why the Church continually urges us to grow in sanctity.

— *RR*

Q. Is purgatory painful?

A. Purgatory is the process after death in which someone who dies in friendship with God is purged of the consequences of sin. We don't have many details of this process in Scripture. But texts that have traditionally been interpreted as allusions to purgatory make it sound as if it's painful. For example:

> If any man's work is burned up, he will suffer loss, though he himself will be saved, but only as through fire.

> — *1 Cor 3:15*

The Fathers and Doctors of the Church who have written about purgatory seem to be largely in agreement that it is extremely painful. St. Augustine said that purgatorial pain is more severe than anything we could possibly suffer in this life. Pope St. Gregory the Great and St. Bonaventure agreed. St. Thomas Aquinas also spoke of the pain of purgatory.

The common conclusion that purgatory involves suffering should not surprise us. God uses adversity in this life to purify us. Purgatory is simply a continuation of that painful trial, presumably more intense and "concentrated."

Nevertheless, we should take consolation in the teaching of the Italian mystic St. Catherine of Genoa (1447-1510), in her *Treatise on Purgatory*. She insisted that the souls in purgatory, though they suffer terribly, are more focused on God than they are on their own sufferings. So despite the pain, they also have marvelous joy.

— *PT*

Q. Do Catholics believe in "the rapture"?

A. The Catholic Church teaches that Jesus Christ "will come again in glory to judge the living and the dead, and his kingdom will have no end," as the Scripture makes clear and as we affirm in the Creed every Sunday. But He will not have an extra, "secret" coming — a "rapture" — to snatch Christians out of the world and leave everyone else to suffer the "great tribulation" of the last days.

The "rapture" notion has never been part of the Church's teaching. None of the Fathers or Doctors of the Church believed in it. In fact, even the Protestant Reformers didn't believe in the rapture. Neither Luther, Calvin, Zwingli, nor later leaders — such as John Wesley — held to that notion. The "rapture" is actually an eccentric idea that developed relatively recently in Church history among a particular group of Christians in England and America. The version, as it's popularly taught today, didn't appear till the 1800s.

The biblical passage most often cited to support this teaching (1 Thess 4:17) doesn't refer at all to a "secret" snatching up of believers. From the earliest centuries, this verse has continually been viewed by serious biblical interpreters — whether Catholic, Orthodox, or Protestant — as a reference to the Second Coming of Christ. At that time, believers will be "caught up" to meet Him as He appears in glory to judge the world and the dead are raised for the final judgment.

— *PT*

Q. Do Catholics believe in the "great tribulation"?

A. As the *Catechism* explains, the Catholic Church affirms:

> … before Christ's second coming the Church must pass through a final trial that will shake the faith of many believers [see Lk 18:8; Mt 24:12].… The Church will enter the glory of the kingdom only through this final Passover, when she will follow her Lord in his death and resurrection.

— *CCC* 675, 677

This period is popularly known as "the great tribulation," based on Jesus' description of it in the Gospel (see Mt 24:21 and the surrounding passage; also Mk 13 and Lk 21).

The *Catechism* speaks as well about the role of the Antichrist in that tribulation:

> The persecution that accompanies [the Church's] pilgrimage on earth [cf. *Lk* 21:12; *Jn* 15:19-20] will unveil the "mystery of iniquity" in the form of a religious deception offering men an apparent solution to their problems at the price of apostasy from the truth. The supreme religious deception is that of the Antichrist, a pseudo-messianism by which man glorifies himself in place of God and of his messiah come in the flesh [cf. 2 *Thess* 5:2-3; 2 *Jn* 7; 1 *Jn* 2:18, 22].
>
> — *CCC* 675
>
> — *PT*

Q. What do Catholics believe about when the final judgment of believers will take place, and whether they will be judged just for their works (see Eph 2:8-9)? Also, who is judged in the "Great White Throne Judgment" (see Rev 20:11-15)?

A. The Church teaches that there are two judgments: the *particular* judgment, which takes place for each individual at the time of death; and the *general* judgment, which will take place at the end of the world and involve all people together. (See *CCC* 1021-1022 and 678-679.) We're speaking here of the *general* (final) judgment of the world.

The Catholic Church affirms (as noted in the Creed) that this last judgment of all people, both believers and non-believers, will take place after Christ's return and the resurrection of the dead. There is no separate "Great White Throne Judgment" for unbelievers at the end of the world. The passage you refer to in the Book of Revelation is simply one of several biblical texts referring to the one final judgment that includes everyone.

Why would some Christians come up with the idea that there are two judgments instead of one? Because several passages in Scripture tell us that in the end, people will be judged according to their works (e.g., Mt 25:31-46; Rev 20:11-15; 2 Cor 5:10), and these passages contradict the common Protestant "faith alone" notion (which implies that God will judge us only according to our faith, not according to our works).

The Scriptural passages themselves contain no evidence of one judgment for believers, according to faith, and a separate judgment for non-believers, according to works. Rather, as St. Paul teaches:

> We must all appear before the judgment seat of Christ, so
> that each one may receive good or evil, according to what
> he has done in the body.

> — 2 Cor 5:10

Some "faith alone" believers have tried to get around this problem by claiming that any biblical description of a judgment according to works must apply to a separate judgment of non-believers, since they insist that believers cannot be judged according to their works. But this is an entirely artificial interpretation imposed on the text.

— PT

Q. What does the Church teach about reincarnation?

A. The *Catechism of the Catholic Church* teaches that death is "the end of man's earthly pilgrimage." It states flatly that "there is no 'reincarnation' after death" (*CCC* 1013).

In Scripture, Hebrews 9:27 says that "it is appointed for men to die once, and after that comes judgment." And as Hebrews 6:2 makes plain, that judgment is "eternal judgment."

— RR

Q. Do ghosts fit into Catholic belief?

Belief in ghosts seems to have been universal across human cultures from the beginning of recorded history, and it's based, at least in part, on countless reports that the living have actually encountered them. Given the special significance that genuine ghostly phenomena would have for theology, Catholics shouldn't so easily dismiss the possibility.

Do ghosts, in fact, exist? To answer that question we must define "ghost."

According to Webster's, the word means "the soul of a dead person, a disembodied spirit." We should keep in mind that in the present discussion, "ghost" does not refer to an angel or demon, a poltergeist, or even an extraterrestrial. Rather, it's that part of a human being which is not corporeal (bodily), and which has been separated from the body through death.

With this definition, Catholics should readily affirm that ghosts do indeed exist. After all, it's a fundamental part of Catholic belief that the human being is a union of soul and body; that at death, the soul and body are separated; and that after death, though the body usually decays, the soul survives, awaiting the Last Judgment, when the body will at last be raised and reunited with the soul.

From a Catholic perspective, then, not only the souls in hell and purgatory, but also the saints in heaven can be called ghosts (with the exception of Our Lady, who is not a disembodied spirit because her body was assumed with her soul into heaven). The question for Catholics is thus not whether ghosts truly exist. They do. The more pressing question is whether disembodied human souls, in the present time before the Last Judgment, are able to manifest themselves to those still alive on earth.

Can the dead appear to the living? Scripture shows that they can. The clearest biblical example of a ghostly apparition is the Gospel account of Our Lord's transfiguration on the mountain, when Moses (who had died centuries before) appeared to Jesus and three of His apostles, conversing with Him (see Mt 17:1-3). We don't include Elijah in this passage as a "ghost" because Scripture seems to indicate that he had not died, but rather had taken his body with him when he left the earth (see 2 Kings 2:11-12).

In the Old Testament, one debated example of a ghostly visitor is that of the deceased prophet Samuel, who appeared to King Saul (see 1 Sam 28:3-20). Some have concluded that the apparition was actually a diabolical counterfeit, since it took place at the bidding of a necromancer (what today would be called a "channeler"), outlawed by God. However, because the Scriptural text itself refers to the spirit repeatedly as Samuel, St. Augustine and other authoritative interpreters have insisted that it was, indeed, his ghost and not a demon.

If we consider as well ghostly visitations in dreams or visions, then we can also cite the biblical story of Judas Maccabeus. He had a vision of Onias, a deceased high priest, praying for the Jews. (This, by the way, is also a Scriptural example of the saints' intercession for the living.) Onias was followed in the vision by the deceased prophet Jeremiah, who spoke to Judas and gave him a golden sword (see 2 Mac 15:11-16).

Beyond the examples in Scripture, numerous accounts of ghostly appearances have come down to us in Catholic tradition since biblical times. Sixth-century Pope St. Gregory the Great, for example, recounted several such instances in his famous *Dialogues*. For Gregory, as for St. Augustine and other Doctors of the Church, ghostly apparitions certainly had their place in a Catholic view of the world.

According to these reports, sometimes the deceased figure who appeared was a recognized saint. At other times, the apparition was of a recently deceased holy man or woman who came to help the living. In still other accounts, a troubled soul — presumably undergoing the purgatorial process — came to ask the help of those still on earth.

No doubt many such stories can be viewed as pious legend, superstition, hoax, or hallucination. But some of them are difficult to dismiss. The more compelling accounts come to us from multiple witnesses of clearly sound mind and impeccable character. These often date from quite recent times and feature first-hand accounts with no possibility of legendary accretions. Among these would be some of the well-known postmortem appearances of St. Pio of Pietrelcina (Padre Pio, 1887-1968).

In the late nineteenth and early twentieth centuries, a number of respected Catholic scholars collected many reliable accounts of ghostly phenomena, gathered from contemporary eyewitnesses and official police and medical documents. A pattern emerges in many of these accounts: when the deceased make an appearance, they often come either to aid the living or to ask the living for help.

How would the dead obtain the power to visit the living? St. Augustine answered simply: "Through God's secret ordinance." It happens with divine permission and through divine power.

And why would God allow ghosts to visit? Apparently, to accomplish spiritual missions for themselves or others.

Finally, we must emphasize that the Church has always forbidden any attempt to *seek out* communication with the dead through means such as "channelers," séances, or Ouija boards. The reason is clear: such attempts to "conjure up the dead... conceal a desire for power... as well as a wish to conciliate hidden powers" (*CCC* 2116).

Dangers abound here: demons can counterfeit the spirits of the deceased, so they may take advantage of these occult practices to manipulate and oppress people. Consequently, we must treat with great caution and discernment any encounters we may have with unexplained phenomena, or reports of such that we may receive from others. Genuine ghostly apparitions, unsought by the living and permitted by God's grace, seem to be extremely rare.

That should be a comforting thought the next time we're alone in the dark....

— PT

Q. What does the Catholic Church think about life on other planets?

A. The possibility of life on other planets has been debated throughout the centuries, but the Catholic Church has never taken an official position on this particular issue. In recent years, remarks from scientists at the Vatican observatory seem to have been quite sympathetic to the notion — but, of course, these scientists don't speak officially for the Church.

"Life on other planets" can refer both to intelligent life and non-intelligent life. The more pressing form of the question is whether extraterrestrial *intelligent* life (ETI) exists. That possibility raises all kinds of interesting speculations about the relationship of such intelligent life to God.

Might some extraterrestrial races be fallen as we are, and others be unfallen? And if some are fallen, would Jesus Christ have a role in their salvation — or, as the second "Adam" (in St. Paul's words [see 1 Cor 15:45]), is He the Savior only for the race of Adam?

This is certainly a subject that calls for further study by theologians.

— PT

3.

Questions about the Sacraments and Liturgy

Q. What is the reason for abstaining from eating or drinking anything one hour before receiving the Eucharist?

A. The Eucharistic fast promotes a deeper reverence and respect for this august sacrament, which is not ordinary food; it is the *panis angelorum*, the "bread of angels." St. John the Baptist prepared the way of the Lord with fasting and penance because fasting makes room in the heart, mind, body, and soul for the Lord. We fast before Holy Communion for the same reason: to prepare the way for the Lord, to make room for Him, to "clean house."

The human body and soul are so closely connected that the soul is prepared for a more fruitful reception of the Blessed Sacrament when the body is denied the comfort and satisfaction of eating or drinking. The one-hour fast increases mental alertness and fosters a deeper hunger in the soul to become united with Our Lord.

The *Code of Canon Law* establishes:

> Whoever is to receive the blessed Eucharist is to abstain for at least one hour before holy communion from all food and drink, with the sole exception of water and medicine.

> — Canon 919.1

But, it notes, this discipline does not apply to the sick and elderly:

> The elderly and those who are suffering from some illness, as well as those who care for them, may receive the blessed

Eucharist even if within the preceding hour they have con-
sumed something.

— Canon 919.3

— *FH*

Q. Why is a selection from the Book of Psalms always included
in the Mass?

A. The lectionary reading in Mass designated as the "Responsorial Psalm" is most often from the Book of Psalms, but not
always. It may be a psalm-like passage from another biblical book.
For example, one of the designated options for the "Responsorial
Psalm" for the Votive Mass of the Sacred Heart (when occurring
during the Easter season) is taken from the twelfth chapter of the
prophet Isaiah.

Even so, the custom of including a "psalm" of some sort in
every Mass goes back to the Jewish roots of Christian worship.
Since ancient times, the Psalms have been the principal "hymn-
book" of the Jewish people, an indispensable part of their liturgy.
Not surprising, then, that since the earliest times of the Church,
this most beautiful of biblical books has been an essential part of
Christian worship.

— *PT*

Q. Is there an automatic dispensation from Sunday Mass for
those who are traveling?

A. No, there is not. Catholics have a serious obligation to
attend Mass on Sundays, not only to keep the Third Commandment, but also to give thanks to God for the many blessings He
sends our way. God asks for only one hour a week from us, and
that's less than 1 percent of the hours in our week.

Only when it is physically or morally impossible for a Catholic to attend Sunday Mass, or for higher reasons of charity (such
as caring for a sick person), is that person exempted from the

Sunday obligation. If people are traveling on Sunday, they should plan in advance.

A convenient resource to help you plan where and when to attend Sunday Mass is www.masstimes.org. All you have to do is enter the name of the town or zip code where you will be, and you will instantly receive a list of all available Masses in the vicinity. I suggest you also call ahead just to confirm that the information is correct.

Also, travelers should be aware that many airports have chapels offering daily Mass.

— *FH*

Q. What is a "Master of Ceremonies" for the Mass, and why do we need one?

A. A good "Master of Ceremonies" is worth his weight in gold, especially if the liturgy is somewhat complicated or solemn, as is the case for confirmations, ordinations, the services of Holy Week, and various large concelebrations. The "Emcee" is in charge of directing and coordinating all the ministers of the liturgy so that the overall effect will be pious, reverent, elegant, and beautiful. Without an "Emcee," some liturgical celebrations could easily disintegrate into a show of clerical "bumper cars" in the sanctuary.

— *FH*

Q. Is it liturgically proper to use recorded music during the Mass to lead the congregation in singing?

A. None of the Church documents that regulate the liturgy specifically prohibit the use of recorded music during the Mass. The 1967 Instruction on Music in the Liturgy, *Musicam Sacram*, as well as the *General Instruction of the Roman Missal* (2002) and the more recent instruction *Redemptionis Sacramentum* (2004), each promote beautiful liturgical music and give pride of place to

Gregorian chant and the pipe organ. But they are silent about the use of recorded music to lead the congregation in singing.

Nevertheless, the use of recorded music is not within the tradition of the liturgy and should not be used to replace the active singing of the faithful, just as it would not be proper to have prerecorded responses of the faithful. Participation has to be actual.

At the same time, if no organist is available and the congregation is musically challenged, a pre-programmed digital electronic organ can be a great help in adding majesty and solemnity to the Mass and could be used as an aid to the singing. This is not prerecorded music, but the use of a pre-programmed instrument for an actual rendition. Whether or not this is "proper" is a matter of opinion, but it is not prohibited.

— FH

Q. Is the *Novus Ordo* liturgy ever celebrated in Latin?

A. Yes, the *Novus Ordo* is sometimes celebrated in Latin. This "Ordinary Form" of the Mass (as opposed to the "Extraordinary Form," or the older, Traditional Latin Mass) is most often heard in the vernacular languages. But the official text on which these vernacular translations are based is itself in Latin, and this text is used whenever the *Novus Ordo* is celebrated in Latin. The *Novus Ordo Missae* (literally, "New Order of the Mass") is the one that is most commonly celebrated today, promulgated by Pope Paul VI in 1969 and published in 1970.

— PT

Q. Why do priests tell their congregations that those who are not Catholic cannot receive Communion?

A. Priests who tell their congregations that "those who are not Catholic cannot receive Communion" are simply speaking the truth and passing along what the Church teaches. Sometimes that position is not very popular and calls for a certain pastoral sensitivity, but it is the right thing to do.

There are some exceptions. The most notable is for members of the Orthodox Churches, who may receive Holy Communion, as well as Penance and Anointing of the Sick, when they request them spontaneously. Outside of exceptional circumstances, clearly defined in canon law, Protestants are not to receive Holy Communion, and in no case are the non-baptized to be allowed to receive the Holy Eucharist.

This disposition is not a lack of friendliness with non-Catholics, but simply the consequence of what it means to receive Holy Communion. That act means the person who receives it assents to everything the Church teaches. Non-Catholics do not.

Holy Communion is also a sign of unity. Most Catholic churches have missalettes in the pews, and most missalettes reprint the USCCB's "Guidelines for the Reception of Holy Communion." In part, they state:

> Because Catholics believe that the celebration of the Eucharist is a sign of the reality of the oneness of faith, life, and worship, members of those churches with whom we are not yet fully united are ordinarily not admitted to holy Communion.

— FH

Q. Are Catholics allowed to receive communion in non-Catholic churches?

A. No, receiving communion in a non-Catholic church would proclaim that a person is in "communion" with that denomination and its teachings, and therefore not in "communion" with the Catholic Church.

Moreover, communion for Protestants is not what it is for Catholics. We believe that Jesus Christ is truly present in the Holy Eucharist (Body, Blood, Soul, and Divinity); He really is present because bishops who enjoy an unbroken continuity with the original apostles, ordained by Christ, have validly ordained our priests. Protestants, on the other hand, do not have the Real

Presence, nor do most of them even believe in the Real Presence in Communion.

The only time that a Catholic may licitly receive the Eucharist in a non-Catholic Church is spelled out clearly in Canon 844.2:

> Whenever necessity requires or a genuine spiritual advantage commends it, and provided the danger of error or indifferentism is avoided, Christ's faithful for whom it is physically or morally impossible to approach a Catholic minister, may lawfully receive the sacraments of penance, the Eucharist and anointing of the sick from non-Catholic ministers *in whose Churches these sacraments are valid* (emphasis added).

It is commonly understood that these sacraments are valid in the Eastern Orthodox churches, as well as the Assyrian Church of the East and the Polish National Catholic Church. But they are not considered valid in the Protestant churches.

— FH

Q. Why do Catholics have to pay for Masses?

A. We don't "pay for Masses" because we cannot possibly afford it, since the value of the Holy Sacrifice of the Mass is *infinite*. But it's good for the faithful to request a Mass for a specific intention, and at the same time, to make an offering to the priest to help support him and the Church.

Each Mass may be offered by the celebrant for one *principal* intention, which is often announced at the Mass. Typically, the intention of the Mass is also printed in the parish bulletin. The intention could be for anyone, living or dead.

Canon law regulates the practice of Mass offerings very closely (see Canons 945-958); even the "appearance of trafficking or trading is to be excluded entirely from the offering for Masses" (Canon 947). The priest is free to accept or decline a request to celebrate a Mass for a specific intention, but once he has accepted it (even if there is no offering), that Mass must be celebrated within one year.

Some priests who have adequate financial support will accept Mass offerings and then distribute them to priests in poorer regions of the world who really need that income. However, it is never appropriate for a priest to deny a sacrament because he would not receive an offering for it.

— FH

Q. If a priest in a state of mortal sin celebrates Mass or provides other sacraments, are they still valid?

A. Yes, they are valid, as long as the minister of the sacrament intends to do what the Church does. The theological principle at work here is *ex opere operato*, explained in the *Catechism of the Catholic Church* this way:

> The sacraments act *ex opere operato* (literally: "by the very fact of the action's being performed"). . . . It follows that "the sacrament is not wrought by the righteousness of either the celebrant or the recipient, but by the power of God." From the moment that a sacrament is celebrated in accordance with the intention of the Church, the power of Christ and His Spirit acts in and through it, independently of the personal holiness of the minister.

— CCC 1128

Nevertheless, the personal holiness and piety of the priest can have a huge impact on the lives of the faithful he serves. For that reason, priests are encouraged to celebrate the holy sacrifice of the Mass daily, go to Confession regularly, and pray frequently.

— FH

Q. When is the proper time for announcements at the end of Mass?

A. Let's take a look at the *General Instruction of the Roman Missal* (n. 90) on this point:

The concluding rites consist of

- brief announcements, if they are necessary;
- the priest's greeting and blessing, which on certain days and occasions is enriched and expressed in the Prayer over the People or another more solemn formula;
- the dismissal of the people by the deacon or the priest, so that each may go out to do good works, praising and blessing God;
- the kissing of the altar by the priest and the deacon, followed by a profound bow to the altar by the priest, the deacon, and the other ministers.

So, the announcements are to be made following the Prayer after Communion, but before the final blessing.

— FH

Q. What is "Gregorian water"?

A. "Gregorian water" is a mixture of water with salt (a symbol of health and preservation), ash (humility), and wine (spiritual abundance and joy). This mixture is blessed by a bishop to be used in the rite of consecrating churches and altars (that is, dedicating them exclusively to divine use).

"Gregorian water" is so named because it was prescribed by Pope St. Gregory the Great (c. 540-604) to be used at the consecration of a church. The act of sprinkling with this water is called *lustration* (from the Latin for "purification").

— PT

Q. What is "Quinquagesima Sunday?"

A. In the old Church liturgical calendar — still observed in the Extraordinary Form of the Mass (celebrated in Latin) — the weeks immediately preceding Lent are observed as a time of preparation for the upcoming penitential season. In ancient times, Christians began their time of abstinence during this period. (By the way, the ancients gave up *all* animal products for the *entire* season of Lent — not just Fridays.)

The last three Sundays before Ash Wednesday are called *Septuagesima* (Latin, "seventieth"), *Sexagesima* ("sixtieth"), and *Quinquagesima* ("fiftieth"). Although the historical origin of these names for these particular Sundays is disputed, the earliest occurrence of the terms in liturgical literature is in the eighth-century Gelasian Sacramentary.

In the traditional Latin Mass, the *Gloria* is omitted on these three Sundays, just as it is throughout Lent in both the Ordinary and the Extraordinary Forms of the Mass. This omission serves as a reminder of the penitential nature of the season.

— PT

Q. Can Christians be baptized more than once?

A. No, it is impossible to be baptized more than once. If one is validly baptized, any further act of baptism is null and void.

— RR

Q. Can children be baptized despite their parents' objection?

A. You can't have a child baptized if his or her parents object. Even if they do not object, there has to be a reasonable hope that the child will be raised as a Catholic. If the parents do not express an "active objection" to baptism, and if they allow you or others to raise the children in the true Faith, bring them to Mass, and prepare them for the other sacraments, then go ahead and have them baptized and raise them in the Faith yourself.

— FH

Q. What is the status of the soul of a child who is stillborn? If the parents are Catholics, is it possible that their intention of baptizing the child after birth would serve as a kind of "baptism of desire" for the child?

A. No one knows for sure, nor are there any official pronouncements on the matter by the Church. But it is possible that the parents' intention of baptizing their child after birth would serve as a kind of "baptism of desire," as you mention. The *Catechism* states:

> As regards children who die without Baptism, the Church can only entrust them to the mercy of God, as she does in her funeral rites for them.

> — *Catechism of the Catholic Church* 1261

I certainly favor that theory, but this is what you would call a disputed question.

— *PT*

Q. Are baptizing and christening the same thing?

A. "Christening" is just another name for infant baptism, though the term is more often used these days among Episcopalians than Catholics. The word is, of course, related to the word "Christian"; the "christening" is so called because it's the occasion when the child receives his or her "Christian" name.

— *PT*

Q. Is baptism using the words "in the name of the Creator, and of the Redeemer, and of the Sanctifier" valid? Where did this formula come from?

A. In February 2008, the Vatican's Congregation for the Doctrine of the Faith (CDF) made public its answer to a question it had received about whether a "baptism" using the formula you note or similar non-standard words ("Creator," "Liberator," "Sustainer") is valid. The answer was a firm no. Pope Benedict XVI approved the CDF document, which was adopted at the ordinary session of the Congregation, and ordered its publication. A note attached to it said in part:

> Baptism conferred in the name of the Father, the Son, and the Holy Spirit obeys Jesus' command as it appears at the end of the Gospel of St. Matthew.... The baptismal formula must be an adequate expression of Trinitarian faith; approximate formulae are unacceptable.
>
> Variations to the baptismal formula — using non-biblical designations of the Divine Persons — as considered in this reply, arise from so-called feminist theology [as an attempt] to avoid using the words Father and Son, which are held to be chauvinistic, substituting them with other names. Such variants, however, undermine faith in the Trinity.
>
> The response of the Congregation for the Doctrine of the Faith constitutes an authentic doctrinal declaration, which has wide-ranging canonical and pastoral effects. Indeed, the reply implicitly affirms that people who have been baptised, or who will in the future be baptised, with the formulae in question have, in reality, not been baptised. Hence, they must then be treated for all canonical and pastoral purposes with the same juridical criteria as people whom the *Code of Canon Law* places in the general category of "non-baptised."

This baptismal formula is an attempt to avoid using the names "Father" and "Son" for the first two Persons of the Blessed Trinity because the more radical feminist theologians — contrary, of course, to all authoritative Catholic tradition — insist that it's illegitimate to use masculine nouns and pronouns to refer to God. This erroneous position implies, of course, that Jesus himself didn't know what He was talking about when He constantly called God "Father."

You have to wonder if these folks believe that Jesus could be wrong about something so central to His mission as revealing the identity of God as Father (see John 17, for example). If so, how could they possibly believe that Jesus was the incarnate Son of God, the Second Person of the Trinity, who had known the Father in perfect communion from before all eternity? How could they possibly trust Him to be their Savior? How could they ever have confidence in anything else He had to say?

— *PT*

Q. What is a good confession? Do you have to be very specific about the type of sin and the number of occurrences?

A. A good confession is an *integral* confession accompanied by genuine sorrow for one's sins and a firm resolution to improve and avoid future occasions of sin. A confession is *integral* if the penitent mentions the number and kind of all mortal sins of which he or she is aware and which have not been previously confessed.

When confessing mortal sins, it is enough to mention the number of times, the nature of the sin, and any aggravating circumstances. An aggravating circumstance would be a situation that made the sin more serious.

For sins against the sixth commandment it is enough to mention, for instance: I committed adultery on two occasions with two different persons; I committed fornication three times. An aggravating circumstance might be the age of the person or relationship of that person to you. Another aggravating circumstance might be intoxication. If you stole something, you should also mention the value of the item, and how you plan to make restitution.

Normally, an experienced confessor might ask some questions to help you be complete and sincere while at the same time avoiding useless questions. For the confessor to give you sound advice, he needs to know the complete picture of your situation, so try to be very sincere. If you are telling too much detail, or useless information, the confessor will politely cut you off and redirect the conversation.

— *FH*

Q. Is following a priest's advice given after Confession mandatory? I recently went to Confession. In addition to giving me a penance, the confessor gave me certain instructions about what I should do. I performed the prescribed penance, which I know I'm obliged to do, but am I also obliged to follow his advice? He told me to do something that seems impossible for me to do.

A. There are five steps to a good confession: examination of conscience; contrition; purpose of amendment; confession; and finally, satisfaction. If you performed the prescribed penance, then you have made "satisfaction," and your confession is complete.

The advice that the confessor gives should be accepted in the spirit in which it is offered: friendly and fatherly advice from a doctor of the soul who wants the best for you. Strictly speaking, it is not necessary to follow the advice, but much depends on the nature and content of the specific advice. It may happen, from time to time, that the advice might not be entirely suited to your condition, but more often than not, the advice is salutary for your soul. Following the advice of the priest may be an indication that the penitent has *true purpose of amendment*, which also indicates sincere *contrition*, a necessary act of the penitent.

I would encourage you to take some time and reflect on that advice in the presence of God and ask the Holy Spirit to help you discern whether you should make a better effort to put that advice into effect. And remember, "All things are possible with God" (Mk 10:27).

— *FH*

Q. Is it possible for an Anglican to go to Confession to a Catholic priest? If so, is the priest obliged to keep such a

confession as private and sacrosanct as he would keep the
confession of a Roman Catholic?

A. Under normal circumstances, a Catholic priest could not
administer Penance to an Anglican, but there are extreme cases
when an Anglican could go to Confession to a Catholic priest.
In such a case, the priest is obliged to keep that confession absolutely secret. Not to do so would be to "break the seal" of the
confessional, which would cause the priest to be automatically
excommunicated, a penalty that could only be lifted by the Holy
See. However, note that this provision is only "if there is danger
of death" or if the bishop decides that there is "some other grave
and pressing need."

This exception is established in Canon 844.4:

> If there is a danger of death or if, in the judgment of the
> diocesan Bishop or of the Bishops' Conference, there is
> some other grave and pressing need, Catholic ministers may
> lawfully administer penance, the Eucharist and anointing
> of the sick to other Christians not in full communion with
> the Catholic Church, who cannot approach a minister
> of their own community and who spontaneously ask for
> them, provided that they demonstrate the Catholic faith in
> respect of these sacraments and are properly disposed.

— *FH*

Q. Is it possible to have Confession en masse?

A. It is already possible to receive General Absolution (Confession en masse) when the circumstances permit it. But generally, circumstances do not permit it. This is outlined in the *Code
of Canon Law*, 961.1:

> General absolution, without prior individual confession,
> cannot be given to a number of penitents together, unless:

1) danger of death threatens and there is not time for the priest or priests to hear the confessions of the individual penitents;

2) there exists a grave necessity, that is, given the number of penitents, there are not enough confessors available properly to hear the individual confessions within an appropriate time, so that without fault of their own the penitents are deprived of the sacramental grace or of holy communion for a lengthy period of time. A sufficient necessity is not, however, considered to exist when confessors cannot be available merely because of a great gathering of penitents, such as can occur on some major feast day or pilgrimage.

It is up to the diocesan bishop and the bishops' conference to determine when the second condition applies. Generally, outside of mission territories, the second condition does not apply at any time in the United States.

— *FH*

Q. In case of emergency (with death imminent), can we listen to someone's confession and forgive his or her sins?

A. No, only a priest has the power to forgive sins through the sacrament of Confession. If a person in danger of death wants his sins forgiven and no priest is available, it is sufficient for that person to make a perfect act of contrition. In that case, the Lord will not deny His mercy, grace, or forgiveness to the person.

If the person insists on confessing his sins to you, politely dissuade him and encourage him to tell them directly to God and have confidence in His mercy. You can help the person by reciting an act of contrition together. However, if the dying person reveals his sins to you, you have the moral obligation to keep them secret.

— *FH*

Q. Are we limited to one saint name at Confirmation?

A. You are not limited to only one, just as John Paul I was not limited to one name when he became Pope.

— FH

Q. Why does the age when Confirmation is allowed seem to vary so widely, even within a particular diocese?

A. According to canon law, Confirmation is to be conferred "on the faithful at about the age of discretion, unless the conference of bishops has determined another age" (Canon 891). In the United States:

> The National Conference of Catholic Bishops authorizes diocesan bishops to determine the age at which the sacrament of confirmation is conferred in their dioceses.

> *— NCCB Complementary Norms*, p. 11

This regulation explains why the age for Confirmation can vary so widely, even within the same diocese: each bishop can decide.

The sacrament of Confirmation strengthens us with the sevenfold gifts of the Holy Spirit, and that bonanza of grace is a good reason to receive Confirmation as soon as possible. However, it's not absolutely necessary for our salvation, and therefore some may find it pastorally appropriate to confirm youths in their teenage years, in order to keep the youngsters enrolled in CCD for a longer period of time.

— FH

Q. If a person receives the sacrament of Confirmation but leaves the Church for a long time, does that person have to receive the sacrament of Confirmation again?

A. The sacraments of the Eucharist, Reconciliation, Matrimony, and Anointing of the Sick can be received more than once.

Confirmation, however, is one of the three sacraments that can be received validly only once.

Why is this the case? Because these three sacraments — Baptism, Confirmation, and Holy Orders — leave an indelible mark on the soul. That is, each of these sacraments imparts to the soul a specific character that will always remain. (See *CCC* 1304-1305.)

For this reason, each person receives Confirmation only once, just as each person is baptized only once, and priests receive Holy Orders (are ordained) only once. There is no need to repeat Confirmation, even if a person has been away from the Church for a long time. Such a person need only return and be reconciled to God and the Church through the sacrament of Reconciliation so that the graces of Confirmation previously received can have their full effect.

— PT

Q. Is the sacrament of Confirmation required before one can marry?

A. It is not an absolute requirement, but it sure helps. Sacraments strengthen us when they are received with faith and devotion. These days, spouses need all the grace and help they can get to shoulder their responsibilities in the married state and remain loving and faithful to each other. The sacrament of Confirmation confers a special outpouring of the Holy Spirit, the Sanctifier of our soul, and bonds us more closely to Christ.

Many couples who have approached matrimony relying on the grace of the sacraments have been blessed with abundant peace and joy on the otherwise "bumpy road of love."

Canon 1065.1 states:

Catholics who have not yet received the sacrament of confirmation are to receive it before being admitted to marriage, if this can be done without grave inconvenience.

Moreover, the spouses are earnestly recommended to make a good confession before they marry.

— FH

Q. Marriage is one of the sacraments that does not have to be conferred by a priest. The individuals getting married confer it upon each other. So is it accurate to say that all marriages, whether by a justice of the peace or a minister of some other denomination, are accepted by the Catholic Church, and the individuals have received the sacrament?

A. No, it is not accurate. As a general rule, a Catholic must marry according to the canonical form of the Church, that is, in the presence of the parish priest and with two witnesses. Anything else would not be valid, unless there was a specific dispensation from canonical form by the competent ecclesiastical authority. And if the marriage is invalid for the Catholic, there is no sacrament. However, non-Catholics can be married validly by a justice of the peace or a minister.

— FH

Q. Can a Catholic who knows that he or she is sterile nevertheless validly contract marriage within the Church, if the spouse-to-be knows the situation?

A. Sterility is not an impediment for marriage, but "antecedent and perpetual impotence" is (Canon 1084). The two are often confused. If the spouse-to-be knows about the other person's sterility, the two can contract marriage validly. However, if the sterile spouse hides the fact of sterility from the other, or if the non-sterile spouse is in error about that quality, such deception or error could be grounds for declaring the marriage null according to Canon 1097.2:

> Error about a quality of the person, even though it be the reason for the contract, does not render a marriage invalid unless this quality is directly and principally intended.

And Canon 1098 states:

> A person contracts invalidly who enters marriage inveigled by deceit, perpetrated in order to secure consent, concerning some quality of the other party, which of its very nature can seriously disrupt the partnership of conjugal life.

— FH

Q. Can a Catholic priest offer the sacrament of Matrimony to a same-sex couple?

A. No, a Catholic priest cannot offer the sacrament of Matrimony to a same-sex couple. Even if he attempted to do so, the marriage would not be valid. Whatever practices civil authorities may choose to legalize under the title of "marriage," in truth a valid marriage is by its very nature limited to the union of one man and one woman. Two people of the same sex simply cannot contract a valid marriage.

— FH

Q. Is an annulment necessary if your first marriage was by a justice of the peace and you now want to be married in the Church?

A. Yes, you still need the annulment. You have to work through your local chancery office, but this kind of case moves quickly. The reason you need the declaration of nullity is that every marriage, in the eyes of the Church, enjoys the favor of the law: it is assumed valid until proved otherwise. If one or both of the parties involved are Catholic, the marriage is *illicit* (that is, not according to canonical form), but it is still *valid*. Moreover, there could be complicating circumstances arising from the first marriage, such as children and other commitments, which might suggest that it not be prudent for the person to attempt another marriage.

— FH

Q. Why are there so many more marriage annulments today than in times past?

A. Definitely, there are more marriage annulments than in the past, especially in the United States, because civil divorce is more common. Given that Catholics want to validly remarry and continue to receive the sacraments, they seek a declaration of nullity for their first marriage. So there are more annulments because there are more civil divorces.

The real question is this: why are there so many civil divorces? Because it's legal? Because of "no-fault" divorce laws? Because of widespread use of contraception? Because of inadequate preparation for marriage? Because most Catholics don't go to Confession? Because of psychological immaturity? Probably all of the above.

As for annulments, in general, American marriage tribunals are staffed by well-trained professionals who take their work seriously, and their definition of a valid marriage is what is stated in the 1983 *Code of Canon Law*. However, Canon 1095.2 provides a ground for nullity ("grave defect of discretion of judgment") that is frequently invoked in declaring a marriage null.

The virtue of Canon 1095.2 is also its vice: it is wide open to interpretation. Some interpret it loosely, others more strictly. One could make the case that it is too easily and too frequently invoked.

In fact, for several years, the late Pope John Paul II lectured the judges of the Roman Rota (the supreme court of the Church) on an annual basis that "difficulties in married life" are not the same as "impediments to a valid marriage." This has led some to conclude that perhaps more annulments than necessary have been granted.

But there are many other reasons why marriages can be nullified, and these are increasingly frequent: lack of canonical form, exclusion of an essential property such as unity or indissolubility, the incapacity to be faithful, grave psychological disorders, the intention of not having children, and so on. However, even if couples do not understand what Christian marriage is all about, "marriage enjoys the favor of the law," which is to say that we always presume a marriage is valid unless proved otherwise.

— *FH*

Q. Can the Church perform a purely sacramental marriage without civil effect?

A. A "secret marriage" without civil effects, or an "extraordinary form" celebration of marriage without civil effects, could be allowed by the local bishop on a case-by-case basis. But currently in the U.S. the bishops have deemed it imprudent to do so. My sense is that it would be illegal according to various state laws throughout the U.S., and for that reason the bishops hesitate. (In some states, it could be a Class 4 felony to marry a couple without a marriage license.)

The priest is not allowed to perform/witness such a marriage without the approval of the bishop. (The relevant canons are Canons 22, 1672, and 1059.)

— *FH*

Q. Can the Last Rites be given to a dying and comatose Catholic patient? What about someone who seems to have expired only moments before the priest arrives?

A. So long as there is some hope that the patient may have wanted to receive the Anointing of the Sick and/or absolution from his sins, a priest may conditionally administer these sacraments to dying and unconscious patients if there is some indication that he might still be alive. Obviously, it is much better to receive these sacraments while the patient is still conscious and better able to profit from the grace. Don't hesitate to call the priest to prepare our brothers and sisters for a holy death.

— *FH*

Q. Can an Alzheimer's patient, who is not in danger of death,
    receive the sacrament of Anointing?

A. Yes, a person with Alzheimer's, who is not in danger of
death, may receive the sacrament of the Anointing of the Sick. It
is best not to delay this sacrament so that the elderly person can
receive it while still in full, or almost completely full, possession
of his or her faculties.

Normally, the fruitful reception of the Anointing of the Sick
is preceded by a good confession, and to make a good confession,
a person should be able to remember his sins, express true contrition, and have a firm purpose of amendment. If the demented
person is largely unaware, frequently incoherent, or otherwise
non-communicative, and if the Anointing of the Sick has not yet
been administered, it should be administered without delay. In
this case, the priest will help the person to express some sign of
sorrow in recognition of past sins, in order to help prepare the
heart and soul to be open to Jesus Christ and His mercy.

— FH

Q. Is blue permitted during Advent in place of the traditional
    purple candles and vestments?

A. Blue, a color traditionally associated with Our Lady, is prescribed as the liturgical color in Spain and some Latin American
countries for the Feast of the Immaculate Conception. It is also
used for other Marian feasts in some Eastern Catholic churches.
But nowhere is blue prescribed in the Roman Rite in the U.S. for
Advent or for any other time.

Nevertheless, some parishes have replaced the traditional
purple furnishings of Advent with blue ones, with various reasons
given for the change. However, purple has an important, specific,
and ancient dual meaning: it is the color both of penance and of
royalty.

It's not surprising, then, that the Church instructs us not to tamper with this and similar aspects of our liturgical customs. When we do, we lose the intended significance of the custom, and we distance ourselves needlessly from earlier generations of the faithful who trusted the wisdom of the Church enough to maintain the tradition faithfully.

The *General Instruction of the Roman Missal* provides the Church's authoritative rules for celebrating Mass. Here's what it has to say about the matter:

> As to the color of sacred vestments, the traditional usage is to be retained: namely... Violet or purple is used in Advent and Lent.... Rose [pink] may be used, where it is the practice, on *Gaudete* Sunday (Third Sunday of Advent) and on *Laetare* Sunday (Fourth Sunday of Lent).

— N. 346

— *PT*

Q. Is it true that the date on which we celebrate Christmas (December 25) has pagan origins?

A. The actual date of Jesus' birth is long lost in the mists of ancient history. The fact that shepherds were "in the fields and keeping the night watch over their flock" (Lk 2:8) suggests that it was springtime. So why did the Church establish the feast of the Nativity on December 25?

The common explanation was propagated by an eighteenth-century German Protestant scholar who sought to prove that the Catholic Church was guilty of various "paganizations." He claimed that, since a pagan Roman feast was celebrated on December 25 in ancient times to honor the sun, the Church decided to co-opt it by having Christians observe Christmas festivities instead.

This claim has been subsequently challenged by historians who believe that events actually developed the other way around.

This date, they insist, had no religious significance in the Roman pagan festal calendar before the year 274, nor did the cult of the sun play a prominent role in Rome before then. Rather, the pagan feast celebrating the "Birth of the Unconquered Sun," instituted by the Roman Emperor Aurelian on December 25 of that year, had political purposes and served to give a pagan significance to a date already important to Roman Christians. Later, Christians in turn re-appropriated the pagan celebration to refer to the birth of Jesus Christ, the "Sun of Salvation" or the "Sun of Justice."

If this is the case, then we still must ask why the early Christians would have chosen the day December 25. According to this historical scenario, they were attempting to calculate the date of Jesus' birth according to the notion, inherited from Jewish religious culture, that a great prophet was destined to die on the same calendar date as that of his birth or conception.

Because of previous calculations involving the ancient Jewish lunar calendar and the date of the Passover, Christians in the West generally came to the conclusion that Jesus had died on March 25, and thus had been conceived on that day as well (which is when we celebrate, of course, the Feast of the Annunciation). Nine months later (December 25) would then have been the reasonable date to set for Jesus' birth.

We might reasonably ask whether it would really matter if either historical scenario were somehow proven conclusively to be true. Even if the Church did arrange its liturgical calendar to "baptize" a pagan holiday (as it seems to have done with All Saints' Day), the legitimacy of the principle has long been established: whether it's evergreen wreaths or wedding rings, the customs of pagan cultures can be fruitfully adopted by the Church, enriched with Christian meaning, and made her own.

— *PT*

Q. Why do we call the day that Jesus was crucified and died "Good Friday"?

A. The origin of the term "Good" in the English name is unclear. Some say it comes originally from "God's Friday" (just as the English word "goodbye" came from "God be with ye"). But that's not its name everywhere. It's known as "Holy and Great Friday" in the Eastern liturgies, and simply "Holy Friday" in Vietnamese, Japanese, and the Romance languages (such as French, Spanish, Portuguese, and Italian). The German name comes from an old term meaning "Lamentation Friday," and it's known as "Passion Friday" in Russian. The Scandinavian peoples (Danish, Swedish, Norwegian, Finnish, Icelandic) refer to it as "Long Friday" — perhaps because fasting makes it seem that way!

In any case, now that the day has come to be called "Good Friday" in English, we can think of this development as providential in light of St. Paul's statement: "We know all things work for *good* for those who love God, who are called according to His purpose" (Rom 8:28, emphasis added). "All things" include Christ's crucifixion — *especially* His crucifixion.

As St. Augustine put it, God allows evil to take place because He can always bring out of it a greater good. From the evil of that day, He brought an infinitely greater good: the redemption of the world. So we remember this day with gratitude, and call it "Good Friday."

— *PT*

Q. Why do Orthodox Christians celebrate Easter on a different day from Catholics and Protestants?

A. The day designated for annually celebrating Our Lord's resurrection varied within the early Church, a situation that sometimes led to controversy. The fathers of the First Council of Nicaea (A.D. 325) recognized that the unity of Catholic faith throughout the world would be better reflected by a consistency in the celebration of this most important of Christian feasts. So they standardized the method for determining its date.

Unlike Christmas, which always occurs on a set date (December 25), Easter was established as a moveable feast, dependent on the shifting relations each year between the cycles of the moon and the sun. The Nicene fathers declared that Easter would fall on the first Sunday after the first full moon to occur after the vernal equinox.

The vernal equinox is the time each spring when the sun crosses the plane of the earth's equator, so that night and day are of approximately equal length all over the world. It usually falls on March 21. Thus Easter never occurs before March 22 or after April 25.

We should note that this not a precise statement of the actual Church rules for determining the date. The full moon involved in calculation is not the astronomical full moon, but rather an "ecclesiastical moon" determined from rather complicated tables developed by the Church. Nevertheless, the ecclesiastical moon keeps in step, more or less, with the astronomical moon.

If the Nicene fathers standardized the celebration of Easter, how is it that Eastern Orthodox Christians usually celebrate on a day different from Catholics and most Protestants? The ancient Nicene rule for calculation is, in fact, still followed essentially by all these Christian communions. But the basic calendar used by the Orthodox churches is itself no longer used in the West.

At the time of Nicaea, the Roman world was using the Julian calendar, so called because it had been introduced by Julius Caesar about 46 B.C. However, the imprecision of this calendar allowed the true (seasonal) year to move away from the calendar year over a period of centuries.

To solve this problem, in 1582 Pope Gregory XIII made adjustments to the Julian calendar to make it correspond more closely to the true length of the solar year. The new arrangement was called the Gregorian calendar.

Catholic countries adopted the Gregorian calendar in 1582, but by that time a discrepancy of ten days had accumulated between it and the Julian calendar. So the extra ten days were eliminated by having the date jump that year straight from October 4 to October 15.

By the early twentieth century, most countries had adopted the Gregorian calendar, at least for secular purposes. Nevertheless, the Eastern Orthodox churches, long separated from papal leadership, continued to use the Julian calendar to calculate the date of Easter. That calendar now runs thirteen days after the Gregorian one.

As a result, Catholics and Orthodox usually end up observing our Lord's resurrection — not to mention the Lenten season and Holy Week preceding it — on different dates.

— PT

Q. What do the letters "P" and "X" on the Easter candle stand for?

A. What looks like "X" and "P" are actually the Greek letters Chi and Rho, respectively. *Chi* (the equivalent of our letter combination "CH") and *Rho* (the equivalent of our letter "R") are the first two letters in the Greek word *Christos*, "Christ."

The *Chi Rho*, as it's called, is thus a symbol of Jesus Christ. In addition to depictions of the two Greek letters side by side, they may be combined artistically in various ways: sometimes with the center of the *Chi* intersecting the leg of the *Rho*; sometimes with the *Rho* forming one of the four arms of the *Chi*.

While we're talking about Christian symbols made of Greek letters, we should note that the "IHS" (also "IHC") sometimes seen in churches is not an abbreviation, as some have suggested, for "In His Service." "I" (the Greek letter *Iota*), "H" (Greek *Eta*) and "S" or "C" (both used for the Greek *Sigma*) are the first three letters of the Greek *Iesous*, or "Jesus."

— PT

Q. What's the difference between All Saints' Day and All Souls' Day? What exactly are we celebrating on these days?

A. On All Saints' Day (Nov. 1), we honor all the saints of God, known and unknown, which means all those who have been fully perfected and united to Him in love in heaven. Though thousands of these holy ones have been formally recognized by the Church and have their own memorial days on the Church calendar, many more have never been canonized. Because of this celebration, the unrecognized saints have a feast day as well — no one is left out!

On All Souls' Day (Nov. 2), we remember all the faithful departed — those who have died in friendship with God but are not yet saints because they are still in the process of being purged and perfected. It's a time not only to remember and honor these Holy Souls in purgatory, but also to offer on their behalf prayers, good works, and the holy sacrifice of the Mass.

— PT

4.

Questions about Our Lady, Saints, Angels, and Demons

Q. Since Jesus is "King of the Universe," doesn't calling Mary "Queen of the Universe" imply that Jesus and Mary are married?

A. You're assuming a regal arrangement in which the queen is the wife of the king, which is how the title is most commonly understood today. Our understanding of Mary's queenship, however, is based on a different arrangement — the one in use during the period of ancient Israel's monarchy. In that kingdom, it was the king's *mother* who reigned as queen, not the king's *wife*.

King David, the shepherd who was anointed to rule God's people, is the forefather of the Good Shepherd, King Jesus, who rules the universe forever. His reign is an Old Testament *type* (or foreshadowing) of Our Lord's eternal reign. Both David and his royal successor, his son Solomon, had multiple wives. But they did not have multiple queens. That honor was reserved for the revered woman who had given birth to the king — the Queen Mother.

The "Great Lady," as she was called, is portrayed in the Old Testament as a preeminent member of the royal court who wore a crown (see Jer 13:18) and headed up the list of palace officials (2 Kings 24:12-15). When the biblical books of 1 and 2 Kings introduce a new king, they almost always mention the name of the queen mother alongside that of her royal son.

In addition, the queen took part in her son's reign. She helped to shepherd the people (see Jer 13:18-20) and was the advocate who presented their petitions to the king (1 Kings 2:17).

Listen to what the angel Gabriel said when he announced to
Our Lady that she would be the mother of Our Lord:

> "And behold, you will conceive in your womb and bear a
> son, and you shall call his name Jesus.... the Lord God will
> give to him the throne of his father David, and he will reign
> over the house of Jacob for ever; and of His kingdom there
> will be no end."

— Lk 1:31-33

When Gabriel announces Our Lord's birth, he is also declaring that Our Lady will be the Queen Mother in Jesus' everlasting
kingdom. Because Jesus is King of the Universe (see 1 Tim 1:17;
6:13-16; Rev 17:14), His mother is Queen of the Universe. As in
all regards, her honor and authority are derived from and dependent on His.

— PT

Q. Why is Mary often depicted with a crown of twelve stars?

A. At one point in his extended vision recorded in the Book
of Revelation, St. John sees "a great sign ... in the sky, a woman
clothed with the sun, with the moon under her feet, and on her
head a crown of twelve stars" (Rev 12:1).

This woman was in labor to give birth to a child that the
devil (pictured as a dragon) wanted to devour, but he failed to do
so. She gave birth to "a son, a male child, destined to rule all the
nations," and he was "caught up to God and His throne" (v. 5).

No doubt you'll see in these words what Christians have long
seen there: who else could be meant by "the male child, destined
to rule the nations," who escaped Satan's attempt to kill him as
an infant, and who later ascended to God's throne in heaven, but
Jesus Christ? And if the Child is Jesus Christ, the woman who
gave birth to Him must be Our Lady. Drawing from the imagery

of this passage, then, Christian artists have often depicted Mary with the crown of twelve stars and the moon under her feet.

We should note that many interpreters have seen the woman in John's vision as a symbol of the nation of Israel, which gave "birth" to the Messiah. But given the Church's affirmation that passages in Scripture may have several layers of meaning — especially ones written in admittedly figurative language, such as this one — then it seems to me that we don't have to choose between those two possibilities. The woman can represent both Mary and God's people; in fact, in Catholic theology, Our Lady herself is viewed as the great representative of God's people.

— *PT*

Q. Why is the color blue often associated with Our Lady?

A. The ancient Egyptians associated the color blue with the sky and the heavens and, by extension, the divine. So far as I can determine, we seem to have inherited this association. Some medieval Jewish rabbis, in fact, spoke of the blue sky as God's throne. In any case, it seems that at least since the early Middle Ages, artistic representations of our Blessed Mother have favored the color blue for her garments.

In modern times the color blue is a common symbol of purity or excellence ("blue-ribbon," "blue chip"). These connotations today enrich the meaning of the association of this color with Our Lady.

Finally, we should note that several alleged apparitions of Our Lady, including Lourdes, describe her as wearing a blue gown, mantle, sash or belt, or bathed in blue light.

— *RR*

Q. What does the "dormition" of Mary mean?

A. *Dormition* is from a Latin word *dormitio,* which literally means "falling asleep." (It's related to our words "dormant" and "dormitory.") It's a figurative term for death (see, for example,

1 Cor 15:18), and it's the preferred term among Eastern Christians (both Catholic and Orthodox) for the event that Latin Rite Catholics celebrate on the Feast of the Assumption of the Blessed Virgin Mary. That feast, and the Eastern "Feast of the Dormition of the *Theotokos*" ("the Mother of God" or, more literally, "the God-Bearer"), are celebrated on the same day (August 15) within the Catholic Church.

Catholic and Orthodox Christians agree that both Mary's soul and her body were taken into heaven, a token of God's promise that He will one day resurrect the bodies of us all. But the difference in these terms reflects a difference in traditions about what exactly happened at the end of Our Lady's life.

In the East, the common belief has been that she died a natural death before her body and soul were taken to heaven. There is a place in Jerusalem known from ancient times as "Mary's Tomb," where she is believed to have been buried in the short interval between her death and her resurrection.

In the West, on the other hand, the question has been left open whether she actually died before she was "assumed," both soul and body, into heaven. When Pope Pius XII promulgated the apostolic constitution that formally defined the dogma of the Assumption (*Munificentissimus Deus*, 1950), his wording allowed for either possibility. It stated that the Blessed Virgin, "having completed the course of her earthly life, was assumed body and soul into heavenly glory." Even so, other remarks in that document imply that Pope Pius himself believed she did, in fact, die.

— *PT*

Q. Was anyone besides Mary assumed into heaven without dying? What happened to Moses, Lazarus the beggar, Enoch, and Elijah?

A. First we should note that Christians have long debated whether Our Lady actually died before she was assumed into heaven. (See the previous question on the dormition of Mary.)

Moses died a natural death. His body was buried in the land of Moab (see Deut 34:5-7; Jude 9), though his spirit showed up again centuries later to speak with Jesus on the Mount of Transfiguration (see Mt 17:1-8).

Most biblical scholars assume the story of the beggar named Lazarus, as told by Our Lord, to be simply a parable He created to teach a spiritual lesson (see Lk 16:19-31). But even if we take Lazarus to be a real historical figure, the story doesn't tell us that he was taken body and soul into heaven. Jesus says, "The poor man died and was carried by the angels to Abraham's bosom" (v. 22). There's little reason to think that these words describe anything more than a natural death, with the soul departing to its proper destination.

We don't really know much about the Old Testament figure named Enoch. He's first mentioned in Genesis 5, along with some of his ancestors and descendants. While the text says about each of the others that they died after living a certain number of years, about Enoch it says instead:

> Thus all the days of Enoch were three hundred and sixty-five years. Enoch walked with God; and he was not, for God took him.
>
> — vv. 23-24

The writer of Hebrews tells us:

> By faith Enoch was taken up so that he should not see death; and he was not found, because God had taken him. Now before he was taken he was attested as having pleased God.
>
> — Heb 11:5

Sirach 44:16 and 49:14 allude to Enoch's special status in this regard as well.

Elijah, the Scripture tells us, was taken up into heaven by a whirlwind on "a chariot of fire and horses of fire" (2 Kings 2:11).

Once he was taken, his companion Elisha "saw him no more" (v. 12); that is, his body was taken as well as his soul.

Both Enoch and Elijah thus seem to have had an experience at least similar to Our Lady's bodily assumption in that, at the end of their earthly lives, their bodies departed from this world as well as their souls. The major difference, however, would be in their immediate destinations.

Our Lady could be assumed body and soul directly into heaven because her Son had by that time accomplished our redemption by His passion, death, and resurrection. But Enoch and Elijah came to the end of their time on earth before those saving events had taken place. So we don't know for sure where they were taken until heaven's doors could be opened for them by Christ. (When the Old Testament text says Elijah was taken up into "heaven," the Hebrew term means what we would call "the heavens" — that is, the sky.)

— *PT*

Q. Did Our Lady ever have to struggle with concupiscence?

A. Concupiscence, the *Catechism of the Catholic Church* tells us, is "human appetites or desires which remain disordered due to the temporal consequences of original sin, which remain even after Baptism, and which produce an inclination to sin" (*CCC Glossary*).

This interior disorder, with which we are all sadly familiar, thus results from original sin. But Our Lady was preserved from original sin by virtue of her Immaculate Conception, so she was not subject to concupiscence — nor was, of course, her divine Son.

— *RR*

Q. How did Our Lady come to be associated with Mount Carmel in the Holy Land? Did she visit there during her earthly life?

A. Carmel is a mountain ridge, about thirteen miles long,

stretching inland from the Mediterranean seacoast, beginning at a point about nine miles southwest of Acre. Its name in Hebrew means "Garden," reflecting its lush vegetation. We have no historical record of Mary visiting that area during her earthly life, though she might well have done so.

The Feast of Our Lady of Mount Carmel, celebrated on July 16, originated with the Order of Our Lady of Mount Carmel, whose origins are somewhat obscure and debated.

From ancient times, religious hermits, seeking to live a life devoted to God, have lived or spent time in the Carmel, which has many caves suitable for dwelling or lodging. Among them was the Old Testament prophet Elijah. After the time of Christ, Christian monks joined other hermits scattered throughout the area. Historical texts show that by the mid-twelfth century, the Carmelite religious order was established there.

About the year 1220 these monks built a chapel in honor of Our Lady, so that they came in time to be called "The Order of Brothers of the Blessed Virgin Mary of Mount Carmel."

The Carmelites initially had many opponents, and it took some time to receive Rome's approval of their work. After Pope Honorarius III formally recognized the rule of the order in 1226, the Carmelites initiated the Feast of Our Lady of Mount Carmel on July 16, sometime between 1376 and 1386. It eventually became the principal feast of the order, whose members, of course, came to spread throughout the world, and the feast was extended to the universal Church in 1726.

The Carmelites maintain a strong Marian devotion, epitomized by the Scapular of Our Lady of Mount Carmel, or the "brown scapular," which is closely associated with St. Simon Stock (c. 1165-1265), a superior general of the order. Among the most famous of the Carmelites are St. Teresa of Ávila, St. John of the Cross, and St. Thérèse of Lisieux.

— *PT*

Q. Why does the Catholic Church use the term "saints" to apply only to those who have been formally canonized? St. Paul in his epistles seems to refer to all Christians as "saints."

A. The Catholic Church doesn't restrict the term "saints" only to those who have been canonized. While she singles out certain persons whose sanctity has been especially noteworthy, she also recognizes that there are countless members of the Church who, in relative obscurity, lived saintly lives and are now with God in heaven. That's one reason we celebrate All Saints' Day: so we can honor all those now in heaven with God, known or unknown to us now.

As for the word St. Paul uses, the New Testament Greek word we translate as "saint" means literally "holy one." In four of his epistles (2 Corinthians, Ephesians, Philippians, Colossians), St. Paul refers to the people of those congregations as "saints" or "holy ones." In two of his epistles (Romans, 1 Corinthians), he addresses himself to all the people, who are "called to be saints" (or "holy ones").

The apostle recognized that by virtue of our baptism and confirmation, we've received the gifts of the Holy Spirit and are God's holy people, called to become perfected in holiness so that we can, in the end, see God face-to-face in heaven. The Catholic Church affirms this truth; in this generic sense, we're all called to be "saints."

At the same time, however, there are Christians whose lives on earth demonstrated exceptional holiness, who even then were "saints" or "holy ones" to an extraordinary degree. When the Church has convincing evidence (miracles through their intercession) that these people are now face-to-`face with God in heaven, she seeks to recognize them in a formal way so that Christians can follow their example and ask for their intercession. It's only reasonable, then, that she would give them the formal title "Saint."

— *PT*

Q. Is canonization infallible? Has the Church ever had to retract a canonization?

A. To answer this question, we must first clarify that the universal Church's formal process of canonization as a part of canon law was not set into place until the thirteenth century. Before that time, the pope and other bishops sometimes formally canonized certain holy men and women. But many of those who came to be designated "saints" in the early centuries gained the title either as faithful characters appearing in Scripture (e.g., St. Lydia), through their prominent leadership and holiness in the life of the Church (e.g., St. Irenaeus), or by popular devotion (e.g., St. Agatha). Most of these early saints were martyrs whose death for their faith gave their contemporaries confidence that they had entered heaven.

Occasionally, the details of the life of one of these earlier saints have come to be viewed as historically uncertain, resulting in some change in the way the Church venerates the saint. Examples of saints with such changes in *"cultus"* would be St. Catherine of Alexandria and St. Christopher. But to my knowledge, Rome has never revoked altogether a formal act of approval it had previously granted for the veneration of such saints.

As for the saints who have been formally canonized by the Church, no canonizations have been "retracted," nor can they be. In fact, according to the Church's Magisterium, the "dogmatic facts" represented by formal canonizations are among those truths "definitively proposed by the Church... Every believer, therefore, is required to give *firm and definitive* assent to these truths" (Congregation for the Doctrine of the Faith, *Doctrinal Commentary on the Concluding Formula of the* Professio Fidei, *1998*, nn. 6, 11; emphasis in the original).

— PT

Q. Why aren't there any Old Testament saints? Didn't biblical persons like Moses, Elijah, or Isaiah fulfill the Church's conditions for canonization — that is, heroic sanctity and performance of at least two miracles? Weren't many of the Old Testament prophets martyrs, and therefore eligible for canonization? Would it be wrong to venerate these Old Testament persons and pray to them for their intercession?

A. It's true there are no feast days for Old Testament saints in the Church's universal calendar. A helpful explanation of this fact has been given by Father Edward McNamara, professor of liturgy at the Regina Apostolorum Pontifical University in Rome. Writing for Zenit News Agency, Father McNamara said the lack is probably due to the way in which the Church's universal calendar was formed.

In the beginning, only martyrs for Christ were honored on the anniversary of their deaths. Soon, feast days for our Blessed Mother began to be observed. This gradual process of development in no way implied we should not ask Old Testament saints to intercede for us.

In fact, the Church does in various ways venerate and ask for the intercession of Old Testament saints. In 1600 a liturgical book, the Roman Martyrology, listed all the saints whom the Church had officially recognized. This listing includes large numbers of saints who do not appear in the Church's general calendar.

The Roman Martyrology remembers, among others, the following Old Testament saints: the prophet Habakkuk (January 15); Isaiah (July 6); Daniel and Elias/Elijah (July 20 and 21); the seven Maccabees and their mother (August 17); Abraham (Oct. 9); and King David (December 29).

Meanwhile, in the litanies of the saints we invoke the prayers of "all holy patriarchs and prophets," who are, of course, Old Testament saints. The first Eucharistic Prayer reminds us of certain outstanding Old Testament figures: "Look with favor on these offerings and accept them as once you accepted the gifts of your servant Abel, the sacrifice of Abraham, our father in faith, and the bread and wine offered by your priest Melchisedech."

In one of the general prayers of the funeral liturgy, we pray, "Hear our prayers and command the soul of your servant N. to dwell with Abraham, your friend, and be raised at last on the great day of judgment."

While the Church in the West recognizes Old Testament saints in these ways, in the Eastern churches, both Catholic and Orthodox, veneration of these holy people is typically more prominent. Witness, for example, the number of Eastern churches named "St. Elias."

Finally, we should note that catalogs selling Catholic religious items sometimes include medals of Old Testament figures referred to as "St. David" and "St. Isaiah."

— *RR*

Q. Could a pope beatify or canonize saintly people who lived before Christ?

A. There is no Church law restricting canonization to persons born in or after the time of Our Lord. However, due to lack of witnesses and information, it seems highly unlikely that a pope would canonize a person from that era.

— *RR*

Q. Is it legitimate to ask a saint to do something other than intercede for us? I thought that the only way saints could help us was through their intercession with God, not through direct action.

A. The notion that the only way the saints can help us is to pass on our requests to God is a common but mistaken idea, not in keeping with Scripture or Tradition. Both Scripture and Tradition tell us that the perfected saints, by God's grace, have come to possess an actual share in His divine power. He is pleased to make it possible for them to help us in many ways — not just through their intercession.

The Scripture tells us that God has made certain "precious and very great promises" through which we will "come to *have a share in the divine nature*" (2 Pet 1:3, 4, emphasis added). This is possible because in Christ, the nature of God himself has been joined to the nature of humanity, and the resulting redeemed human nature, which is "in Christ," now has new possibilities.

We must not limit God by presuming that He is somehow incapable of sharing His power with those who are in Christ. We already see glimpses of His ability and, indeed, His readiness to do so in the lives of certain saints while they still walked the earth. Many of them accomplished deeds and possessed knowledge far beyond what was proper to their human nature, because God's grace was already at work to share with them His divine nature. Scripture, in fact, speaks of how "God has appointed in the Church... workers of miracles" (1 Cor 12:28, RSV).

St. Thomas Aquinas, in his *Disputed Questions on the Power of God* (*Quaestiones disputatae de potentia dei*, Q. 6, Art. 4) touches on this matter. He first notes that St. Augustine had wrestled with the question, prompted by several miracles that took place in association with the relics of certain saints. It was obvious to Augustine that, ultimately, God had worked the miracles, but it was unclear whether He had accomplished them "by himself . . . or by His ministers, or by the souls of the martyrs [saints]."

Thomas goes on to note, however, that Pope St. Gregory the Great (in his *Dialogues* ii, 31) had given "a decisive answer to the question":

> He says that holy men even in this life work miracles not merely by prayer and impetration [intercession] but also authoritatively, and therefore by cooperation: and he proves this both by reason and by examples.
>
> His reason is that if men were given the power to

become sons of God [see Jn 1:12], it is not strange that by that power they can work miracles.

The examples he offers are that of Peter, who without any previous prayer, pronounced sentence of death on the lying Ananias and Sapphira by mere denunciation (Acts 5:4, 9); and of the Blessed [St.] Benedict, who "looked on the bonds of a poor countryman and thus loosed them more speedily than it were possible to human hands." Wherefore he concludes that the saints work miracles sometimes by prayer, sometimes by power.

[Thomas' conclusion is:] It is true that God alone works miracles by His authority [that is, "by His sole command"]; and it is also true that He communicates to creatures the power to work miracles, according to the creatures' capacity and the order of divine wisdom: to the effect that a creature may work a miracle ministerially by grace.

It's simply another instance of the sacramental principle by which God so often operates.

— *PT*

Q. Did any of the saints have a sense of humor? Sometimes when I see so many dour-faced portraits of them, I wonder.

A. The short answer is yes.

From the early centuries of the Church, we might recall the martyr St. Lawrence. Because he refused to renounce his faith in Christ, Roman imperial officials ordered him to be roasted alive, slowly, on a red-hot griddle. According to a popular legend, at one point as he roasted, he said to his torturers: "You can turn me over now. I'm done on this side!"

I think also of St. Francis of Assisi, whom Chesterton has rightly called "the court fool of the King of Paradise." His entire adult life, it seems, was a startling comic elaboration of Christ's act of overturning the tables, smiling playfully as he did so, and pointing out the absurd incongruities of his contemporaries.

Or what about St. Teresa of Ávila? What a quick wit shines through her writings and sparkles in the anecdotes of her biographers! Perhaps you've heard, for example, of how she was on her way one day to perform her administrative duties at one of the religious communities she supervised, when the donkey she was riding on stumbled as it forded a stream, and she was thrown into the muddy water. As she picked herself up and wiped off the mud, she was heard to say with a sigh, "Lord, if this is how you treat your friends, no wonder you have so few of them!"

— *PT*

Q. We need to sell our home. A Catholic friend has suggested we bury a statue of St. Joseph in the yard upside down. Does burying a statue of St. Joseph help sell a house?

A. St. Joseph is, of course, the patron saint of the home, so that probably explains the origins of this custom. Some folks view it as a form of superstition, and some folks sure seem to perform the act in a superstitious way, as if it works magically. But that's the case with many Catholic devotions, even ones that are clearly endorsed by the Church.

I think it all depends on how you approach the matter. If you are tempted to think the statue is "magical," guaranteed to "work," then I'd say don't do it. Just ask St. Joseph to help you.

On the other hand, if you are seeking the saint's intercession; if you view this act as what I would call a kind of "concrete prayer" — that is, a meaningful action that symbolizes and embodies a petition made in faith; and if you recognize that the prayer may not be answered in the way you hope for; then I don't see any problem with burying the statue.

Once the prayer has been answered, I'd encourage you then to follow up by excavating the statue, cleaning it up and placing it in a prominent place in your new home, to remind you to be grateful for St. Joseph's assistance. I would take the same approach, for example, to placing a coin under a statue of the Holy Infant of Prague to ask Our Lord for financial provision.

— PT

Q. Was St. John the Baptist immaculately conceived like Mary? When the angel Gabriel appears to Zechariah and tells him about the birth of John the Baptist (Lk 1:15), he says, "and he [John] will be filled with the Holy Spirit, even from his mother's womb." One commentary on this passage states: "To prepare Israel for the Lord, the Lord first prepares John with grace. He and the Virgin Mary were sanctified before birth." This seems to imply that John was full of grace just like Mary, the equivalent of the Immaculate Conception.

A. In interpreting this Gospel passage, we need to keep several things in mind. First, we shouldn't assume that someone was sinless and "full of grace" in the same sense Our Lady was, just because the Scripture says that the person was "filled with the Holy Spirit." Our Lady's privilege in this regard, through the merits of her divine Son, was unique.

Other characters in the New Testament were also said to be "filled with the Holy Spirit" at various times, with no suggestion or even implication that they shared Mary's privilege. In that same chapter of Luke, for example, Elizabeth herself was "filled with the Holy Spirit" when John leaped in her womb (v. 41). The apostles were all "filled with the Holy Spirit" (Acts 2:4; 4:31), as was St. Peter (Acts 4:8) and St. Paul (Acts 9:17; 13:9). In fact, St. Paul tells us all to be "filled with the Spirit" (Eph 5:18).

Nevertheless, the commentary you cite is probably alluding to the ancient teaching that St. John was in a special category in this regard: he was sanctified *in the womb* at the moment he leaped for joy when his mother, Elizabeth, met Jesus' mother at the Visitation. In that case, both Mary and John were sanctified before their birth.

The Church's liturgy reflects this special status. There are only two saints whose *nativities* we celebrate as universal liturgical feasts: John and Mary.

Nevertheless, there's an important difference between the two here. Conception and birth are not at all the same thing. Our Lady was preserved from original sin from the first moment of her *conception* — from the very beginning of her existence. John, however, was not *conceived* without sin as she was.

According to the ancient teaching, John was *born* without sin. Though he was conceived in original sin, he was sanctified months later by the Holy Spirit before he was born, while still in Elizabeth's womb (as if he were baptized in the womb).

Of course, the other great difference between the two is that Our Lady was preserved as well from all actual sin throughout her life, while John was not.

— PT

Q. One of the recent readings in Mass referred to Mark as Peter's son (1 Pet 5:13). Now I know St. Peter used "son" as an affectionate term, but it made me think. We know St. Peter had a mother-in-law. Did St. Peter have any children?

A. We read that Peter's mother-in-law was healed by Jesus in Mark 1:29-31. The Gospel account tells us that immediately she assumed the duties of hospitality for Jesus and the other guests. These are duties that a wife would normally carry out. This detail in the account suggests, but only suggests, that Peter's wife may not have been living at that point. We know nothing about any children of his.

Luke 18:28-30 seems to tell us something more about Peter's marital status. "And Peter said, 'Lo, *we have left our homes* and followed you.'" Impetuous Peter, the one always blurting out his thoughts, practically demanded to know what would become of him and the other apostles. Jesus replied, "Truly, I say to you, there is no man who has left house or *wife* or brothers or parents or *children*, for the sake of the kingdom of God, who will not receive manifold more in this time, and in the age to come eternal life" (emphases added).

Addressed not only to Peter but also to the other apostles, Jesus' words seem to imply that all the apostles were now living celibate lives as they followed Him in being prepared to become His successors.

— *RR*

Q. Why is St. Timothy the patron saint of those with stomach disorders?

A. St. Timothy, who shares a feast day with St. Titus on January 25, was a young disciple of St. Paul; the apostle apparently loved and trusted him deeply. He is mentioned as a friend and companion of Paul in a number of biblical passages (see, for example, Acts 16:1; Rom 16:21; 1 Cor 4:17), and the two books of the New Testament that carry his name (1 and 2 Timothy) are letters addressed to him from St. Paul.

In his first letter to St. Timothy, St. Paul advised him: "No longer drink only water, but use a little wine for the sake of your stomach and your frequent ailments" (1 Tim 5:23). No doubt Timothy's role as patron saint of those with stomach disorders developed as a result of this biblical passage. According to the ancient Roman Martyrology, St. Timothy became bishop of Ephesus, and he died in his eighties after being beaten by pagan attackers.

— *PT*

Q. How did a breed of dogs come to be named for St. Bernard of Clairvaux?

A. Actually, this giant, lovable dog is named for a different St. Bernard — St. Bernard de Montjoux (c. 996-1081), an Italian priest and monk who did missionary work in the Alps, building churches and schools. He also founded two Swiss Alpine hospices to help weary and lost travelers in the mountain passes that came to be called the Great Bernard and the Little Bernard after him. Pope Pius XI declared Bernard the patron saint of the Alps in 1923.

The Great St. Bernard Pass, as it is now called, is 8,100 feet high and runs through the Valais Alps in Switzerland. It is an ancient route, used as far back as the Bronze Age, with surviving relics of a Roman road. The hospice built there in 1049 by Bernard, also called by his name, offered aid to travelers facing the dangers of robbers, rough terrain, avalanches, and storms on their way between Italy and Switzerland.

This hospice later became famous for the dogs that took its name. "St. Bernards" actually developed in the valley below the pass. They were probably descended from the Molossus breed brought there by the Romans and interbred with local dogs. These large canines were originally used as guard dogs and draft animals on dairy farms and were probably brought back up to the pass by visiting monks. Though St. Bernards made excellent guards and companions for the monks, they came to excel as rescue dogs.

The "other" St. Bernard of Clairvaux (1090-1153) was a Cistercian abbot, mystical theologian, and Doctor of the Church whose influence throughout the religious and political realms of Western Europe in his day was unparalleled.

— PT

Q. Can human beings become angels after they die? Can angels come to earth and become human?

A. The answer to both questions is no. Angels and human beings were created by God as different species; in fact, St. Thomas Aquinas tells us that each angel is its own species!

An angel (even a fallen angel) remains an angel for eternity. A human being remains a human being for eternity as well — though, if he dies in friendship with God, his humanity will be joined to Christ's divinity in such a way that he'll be not only human, but much more as well.

In popular culture such as cartoons and films, people are often depicted as becoming angels. Think of the character named "Clarence" in the Christmas classic *It's a Wonderful Life*, who once lived as a human on earth but now must "earn his wings" to become an angel fully in heaven. Such notions may be whimsical and charming, but they are mistaken. Human beings who go to heaven to live with God aren't angels; they are *saints*. They have become perfected and are enjoying glorious eternal fellowship with God, His angels, and His other saints.

— *PT*

Q. Why do we refer to St. Michael the Archangel, St. Gabriel, and St. Raphael as saints, since all are known to be angels?

A. The confusion arises from the fact that the word "saint" literally means "holy one," and it can have either that general meaning (applicable to any person who is holy: human or angel) or the more specialized meaning of a perfected human being enjoying the Beatific Vision in heaven. In the New Testament, the Greek term is *hagios* (feminine, *hagia*), and the equivalent Latin term is *sanctus* (feminine, *sancta*), from which we derive the English word *saint*.

In Latin, then, the three archangels whose names we know from Scripture are referred to as "Sanctus Michael," "Sanctus Gabriel," and "Sanctus Raphael," in the general sense: "Holy Michael," "Holy Gabriel," and "Holy Raphael." When those names came into English, the "Sanctus" was translated as "Saint" rather than "Holy."

— *PT*

Q. What exactly is an archangel?

A. The word "angel" means "messenger." The prefix "arch-" means "first" or "principal." Hence the term *archangel* means "principal messenger." It occurs in Scripture twice: in Jude 9 ("the archangel Michael") and 1 Thessalonians 4:15 ("the voice of an archangel").

Ancient Christian tradition, drawing in part from even earlier Jewish tradition, holds that the angels form a hierarchy — that is, they are organized in higher and lower ranks, with each rank having distinctive functions. Various descriptive terms are used for angels in Scripture, so Christian writers have attempted since the early centuries of the Church to discern the hierarchical arrangement implied by these terms.

The Old Testament refers to angelic beings called in Hebrew *cherubim* (singular, *cherub*) and *seraphim* (singular, *seraph*). God stationed cherubim to guard the Garden of Eden after the fall of Adam and Eve (Gen 3:24). They are described at length in the prophetic visions of Ezekiel (according to the intriguing form in which they appeared to him [see Ezek 1, 10]).

God commanded the ancient Israelites to make images of the cherubim to adorn the Ark of the Covenant (see Ex 25, 26, 36, 37) and later the temple (see, for example, 1 Kings 6-8). The Psalmist speaks of God as "riding" the cherubim and being "enthroned" upon the cherubim (see Pss 18:11; 80:2; 99:1).

The seraphim are mentioned only in the Book of Isaiah (6). In the prophet's vision, they surround God's heavenly throne and take a form with faces, feet, and six wings.

In the New Testament, St. Paul seems to speak of angelic ranks (Eph 1:21) when he says that Christ is seated at the Father's right hand far above "every principality, power, virtue and dominion" (using the older English terms). Again, in Colossians 1:16, among the things "invisible" he names "thrones or dominations, or principalities or powers."

Finally, we have biblical references to seven angels whose special function it is to "stand before God's throne" (see Tob 12:15; Rev 8-11). The archangel Raphael identifies himself as one of these seven, and the archangel Gabriel appears to do so as well (see Lk 1:19). Tradition counts the archangel Michael among these as well, and the ancient Book of Enoch (which is not a part of Scripture) claims to identify the other four as Uriel, Raguel, Sariel, and Jeramial.

The ancient author now known as Pseudo-Dionysius wrote extensively about the heavenly ranks, or "choirs," as they came to be called. Later, St. Gregory the Great and St. Thomas Aquinas also wrote about them. St. Thomas concluded that there are nine orders of angels, arranged within three hierarchies, distinguished by their proximity to the throne of God.

In the first hierarchy (closest to God), Thomas places the seraphim, cherubim, and thrones. In the second, he envisions (again, using the more traditional English terms) dominations, virtues, and powers. In the third are principalities, archangels, and angels. Thus he taught that the archangels are the next-to-the-lowest rank, just above the angels.

Keep in mind that though the existence of angels is binding on our faith, the existence of the nine orders of angels and their ranks is not. In addition, great Christian teachers have disagreed about where an archangel such as Michael might actually rank within this arrangement.

— PT

Q. How much do we really know about the archangels Michael, Gabriel, and Raphael?

A. Let's begin with *Michael*. In Hebrew, his name means "Who is like God?" The book of Jude identifies St. Michael specifically as an archangel (Jude 9), who is engaged in a dispute with the devil.

Other biblical references confirm that he is "one of the chief princes" of the angels, the "guardian" of God's people who does spiritual battle on their behalf, especially in the days leading up to the end of the world (see Dan 10:12-13, 20-21; 12:1-3). He is also depicted in the Book of Revelation as battling, with his angel troops, against Satan and his fallen angelic allies, finally casting them out of heaven (Rev 12:7-9).

132 Catholic Answers to Catholic Questions

Some of the Church Fathers speculated that Michael might have been the angel God set at the gates of Eden to guard the tree of life (Gen 3:24); the angel through whom God delivered the Ten Commandments (Ex 23:20-23; Acts 7:53); the angel who stood in the way of Balaam (Num 22:22-35); and the angel who routed the army of Sennacharib (2 Kings 19:35).

In light of these biblical texts, Catholic tradition has spoken of four offices of Michael: to fight against Satan; to rescue the souls of the faithful from the power of the enemy — especially at the hour of death; to be the champion of God's people; and to bring souls to judgment.

Opinions have varied about where exactly St. Michael ranks among the angels. St. Basil and other Church Fathers, as well as St. Robert Bellarmine, believed that he is prince over all the angels. Others concluded that he is prince of the seraphim (the first of the nine angelic orders). St. Thomas was convinced that he is prince of the lowest celestial order, the angels.

Whatever the exact nature of his rank and function, St. Michael is a magnificent protector, worthy of our honor and gratitude.

Gabriel, in Hebrew, means "man of God" or "might of God." Several of his appearances are noted in Scripture. In Daniel 8 and 9, he explains the meaning of the prophet's visions. In Daniel 10, he is presumably the angel who tells Daniel how St. Michael came to his aid in answering the prophet's prayer.

Gabriel is best known to Christians, of course, through his role in events surrounding the birth of Our Lord. According to St. Luke, he foretold to Zachariah the birth of St. John the Baptist. Then, he announced to Our Lady the Incarnation of the Son of God in her womb (see Lk 1:5-20, 26-38).

Gabriel is never identified by name in the Gospel of Matthew. But because of his role in the Annunciation, many Christians have assumed that he was also the angel who, according to that Gospel, appeared to St. Joseph in a dream (see Mt 1:20-24).

In both Old and New Testaments, then, Gabriel seems to have a role as God's special herald or messenger — which is, in fact, what the Greek word *angelos* literally means.

Raphael literally means "God has healed." In Scripture he appears by name only in the Book of Tobit, where he speaks of himself as "one of the seven angels who enter and serve before the Glory of the Lord" (Tob 12:15; see also Rev 8:2). His activities as described in that book (see chapters 5-12) include healing, interceding, testing hearts, and battling demons.

The "angel of the Lord" mentioned in some ancient manuscripts of John 5:3 had a role in healing the sick. For that reason, many scriptural commentators have speculated that he was, in fact, St. Raphael. A note: Protestant Christians are often unfamiliar with St. Raphael because their Bible is missing the book (Tobit) that tells about him.

— PT

Q. Who is the archangel Ariel?

A. The only three angels whose names are known in Scripture and firmly established in the Catholic tradition are Michael, Gabriel, and Raphael. Ariel is not among them.

Biblical scholars suggest that the Hebrew name "Ariel" means either "lion of God" or "hearth of God" (the latter applying to a part of the altar in the temple at Jerusalem; see Ezek 43:15-16). The term appears in Scripture, but not as the name of an angel. Ezra 8:16 mentions a man named Ariel in a list of "men of insight," and the prophet Isaiah uses it as a symbolic name for the city of Jerusalem (see Is 29:1, 2, 7).

By the time the Jewish people returned to Israel from their exile in Babylon (in the fifth and sixth centuries B.C.), the rabbinical teaching that had developed apparently included a speculative tradition about the names and special roles of angels, perhaps influenced by pagan Babylonian traditions. "Ariel," "Uriel," and other names eventually began appearing in apocryphal literature as names of archangels.

As early as the second century, St. Irenaeus tells us, the name Ariel had already been appropriated by the Gnostics (an early heretical movement) to identify one of the multitude of "aeons," or spiritual powers, in their mythology (see his *Refutation of All Heresies*, V, 9). Since that time, Ariel and other speculative "angel" names have been used by the Gnostics' spiritual descendants, such as Kabbalists and New Agers.

— PT

Q. Are guardian angels real, or just a fairy tale?

A. It's a part of our Catholic faith that angels exist and have a general role as our appointed guardians. But the doctrine that each individual human being has his own individual guardian angel has never been formally defined by the Church.

Even so, the *Catechism of the Catholic Church* sums up the matter this way:

> From infancy to death human life is surrounded by [the angels'] watchful care and intercession. "Beside each believer stands an angel as protector and shepherd leading him to life."

— CCC 336

Origen (d. c. 254) taught: "Each of us, even the lowliest, has an angel by his side." St. John Chrysostom (347-407) insisted: "Each faithful Christian has an angel." St. Jerome (c. 342-420) declared: "The dignity of a soul is so great that each one has a guardian angel from its birth." St. Ambrose (c. 340-97) counseled: "We should pray to the angels who are given to us as guardians."

The famed Spanish Jesuit theologian Francisco Suarez (1548-1617) put it this way:

> Although not expressly contained in Holy Scripture, nor

yet formally defined, [this doctrine] is received by universal consent in the Church and has such a solid foundation in Scripture, as interpreted by the Fathers, that it cannot be denied without temerity and even error.

— *De Angelis* 6:17

Throughout Scripture we find passages hinting or implying that individual souls have angels who guard and protect them. "God commands the angels," the psalmist says, "to guard you in all your ways" (Ps 91:11; also quoted by Jesus). "The angel of the Lord, who encamps with them, delivers all who fear God" (Ps 34:8). Abraham sent out his steward to seek a wife for his son Isaac with the promise, "He will send His angel before you" (Gen 24:7).

Jesus' words echo these passages:

"See that you do not despise one of these little ones, for I say to you that their angels in heaven always look upon the face of my heavenly Father."

— Mt 18:10, NAB

These biblical texts and others (for example, 1 Kings 19:5; Acts 12:7-11) don't spell out the doctrine that every individual has a guardian angel. But, as Suarez noted, Christians since early times have drawn that conclusion from these passages.

— *PT*

Q. Can the devil create new things?

A. Only God can create things *ex nihilo* (out of nothing). Neither angels (fallen or unfallen) nor human beings can do that. However, human beings, made in the image of God, can through their righteous labors "prolong the work of creation." "By means of his labor man participates in the work of creation" (*CCC* 2427, 2460).

The "labors" of the devil, on the other hand, don't participate in God's work of creation as righteous human labors do. Rather than create, the devil seeks to counterfeit, maim, pervert, and distort God's creations.

— *PT*

Q. Can the devil torment you in your dreams?

A. I don't know that the Church has ever given a definitive answer to that question. We do know from precedents in Scripture that angels can appear to people in their dreams, sent by God. The most famous examples of that occurrence, of course, are St. Joseph's dreams, which instructed him how to care for Mary and Jesus (see Mt 1:21-24; 2:13). Since demons are fallen angels, perhaps they have retained the power, even after their fall from grace, to influence our dreams in some way.

The great medieval theologian St. Thomas Aquinas took this position. In his great work the *Summa Theologiae*, he wrote that "dreams may be caused by spiritual agents, such as God, directly, or indirectly through his angels, and the devil" (II-I:95:6). He also warned that demons may communicate in dreams to those who have sought dealings with them.

A thirteenth-century collection of stories about St. Dominic that claims to be based on information from the saints' companions tells how Dominic once encountered the devil prowling around the convent. When the saint asked him what kind of mischief he accomplished in the dormitory, the demon replied, "I keep the brethren from enjoying their rest, and then tempt them not to rise for matins, and when this does not work, I send them foul dreams and illusions."

The story may be only a legend, but it at least reflects, presumably, a popular belief that the devil could trouble people through dreams. We might note as well that the sixth-century Pope St. Gregory the Great, in his *Dialogues* (II, 8), says of St. Benedict:

The old enemy of mankind [that is, the devil], not taking this in good spirit, presented himself to the eyes of that Holy Father, not privately or in a dream, but in open sight.

The implication here seems to be that the devil was known to appear in dreams.

Even so, I don't think you should automatically assume that a bad dream, even a terrible nightmare, has a supernatural cause. Psychologists who study dreams have confirmed what common sense suggests: most dreams appear to have very natural origins in our personal experience. They are often attempts by the subconscious mind to work through issues of one sort or another. If you feel tormented by dreams, I would suggest that you seek help from your priest, spiritual director, or other trusted counselor.

— PT

Q. Would it make any sense to pray for the conversion of the devil? He is the main cause of human sins. Maybe if we pray for that, everybody would be close to God.

A. It would certainly make sense to pray for the devil's conversion if there were any chance of his converting. But the Church clearly teaches that unlike human beings, the devil (and all the demons) no longer have the possibility of salvation.

The choice they made against God long ago was definitive and irrevocable; they will never repent and turn back to God. (See *CCC* 391-393.) So the devil cannot be converted, and it's useless for us to pray for his conversion.

The situation is similar for human beings who have died rejecting God. Up until death they had the chance to repent and be saved, even if it meant undergoing a considerable purging to prepare them for heaven. But once such people died (rejecting God), they no longer had the chance to be saved; they had made a decision that can never be changed.

We should nevertheless note that the Church teaches that we

cannot know for sure in any given case whether someone who died has gone to hell. So even in the most discouraging of circumstances, we should pray for the dead in the hope that God granted them one final chance to repent and die in His friendship.

— *PT*

Q. Do the good angels still have the capacity to choose against God and become demons?

A. The Catholic tradition has long affirmed that the choices of all the angels, whether for or against God, cannot be reversed. The angels' initial act of free will has been ratified or (in theological terms) "confirmed" by God as permanent, just as, in the case of human beings, God confirms our free will choice for or against Him at death.

The great medieval theologian St. Thomas Aquinas sums up the Church's teaching in his *Compendium of Theology*, when he says:

> The wills of human souls receive confirmation [from God] in good or obstinacy in evil when they are separated from their bodies [at death];... whereas angels were immediately made blessed or eternally wretched as soon as, with full deliberation of will, they fixed upon [either] God or some created good [instead] as their end [that is, the ultimate purpose of their existence].

— N. 184

Why would it be just for God to refuse to give the angels, so to speak, a "second chance"? Because their situation at the time of their choice was quite different from ours.

As Catholic philosopher and apologist Dr. Peter Kreeft has put it, the rebellion of the fallen angels was a choice "made with their whole mind and free will, which they could never take back because there was no ignorance, no temptation, no excuse, and no part of the self holding back" (*Angels and Demons: What Do We Really Know About Them?*, Ignatius, 1995, p. 116).

This truth about the good angels should bring us great assurance. We never have to worry about whether St. Michael, our guardian angels and all the heavenly hosts will one day go over to the "dark side" and try to take us with them.

— PT

5.

Questions about Catholic Practices

Q. What are the differences among various kinds of prayer such as formal, vocal, mental, discursive, and contemplative?

A. First, we should note that the Church embraces all these types of prayer. God welcomes all our efforts to commune with Him, and invites us to delve more and more deeply into the mystery that is prayer.

Formal prayer is prayer with a set *form* — that is, the words prayed have been previously composed (given to us, for example, in the liturgy or through devotional tradition) rather than spontaneously offered by the one praying.

The benefits of formal prayer are many: it allows us to pray in unison (even when we pray alone) with all the other Christians who use the same prayer, throughout the world, across the generations, in heaven as well as on earth. According to Scripture, one example of the latter would be the opening words of the *Sanctus* of the Mass (see Is 6:3; Rev 4:8).

Formal prayer also provides us with thoughts and words we may be lacking when we pray spontaneously. It helps us fill in the "gaps" of our informal prayer, reminding us of concerns we may have neglected. It can allow us to express ourselves more precisely (and sometimes more concisely) in our conversations with God. And it models for us the proper attitudes of prayer.

Vocal prayer (prayer of the voice) is prayer that is spoken aloud. This outward action expresses the internal intention that is essential to prayer. Vocal prayer often, but not always, consists of the reading or recitation of a formal prayer.

Though some Christians have looked down on vocal prayer as a "lower" form of conversation with God, it's quite valuable in that it involves the whole person, body as well as spirit, and it allows prayers to be prayed in common with others. The supreme form of vocal prayer, of course, is the Church's liturgy, the voice of the Bride of Christ speaking to her Lord.

Mental prayer (prayer of the mind) refers to all kinds of prayer other than vocal. It's a direct exercise of the mind and will. Mental prayer includes forms of prayer such as meditation and contemplation.

Meditation (or *discursive prayer*) involves reasoning or reflection on a given subject with the intention of stirring up the will to make acts of faith, hope, love, and humility; and to form godly resolutions.

Contemplation is more difficult to describe without resorting to figurative language. It's a kind of prayer that dispenses with reasoning or discourse in order to concentrate simply and fully on God. Through what might be called a "gazing" on Him with the "eyes" of the soul, the person in contemplation offers up a wordless act of love to the Lord, while the mind and will are utterly engrossed in God and enthralled by God.

— *PT*

Q. Is prayer more effective if it is limited in scope? For example, I can pray for the healing of those who are sick in my parish, or I can pray for the healing of all sick people in the world. If I do the latter, have I "diluted" my prayer such that it's less effective for those in my parish?

A. Now, that's an intriguing question!

In reply, I think the first thing we must note is that prayer is a *mystery* with regard to the ways it actually works. That is, the intricate, complex, often hidden ways in which God responds to a prayer — and the subtle ways in which it affects the one praying as well as the one being prayed for — are beyond our full knowing or understanding.

We can't think of prayer so much in mechanical terms. It's not as if we can apply this much pressure to this wheel, and it turns this fast, but if we apply pressure to several wheels at once, they all turn, but more slowly. In addition, we must keep in mind that prayer is much more than petition (asking for something), including intercession (asking for something for someone else).

Having said all that (and at the risk of still sounding too "mechanical"), I think it's reasonable to assume that a more general prayer is no less powerful in its total effect, but the power is "distributed" in a different way. When we pray for the sick of all the world, we join others around the globe who are also praying that prayer, and the cumulative effects of our prayers are powerful indeed for all the millions of people in our intentions.

On the other hand, when we pray more specifically, we bring to our task all the benefits of greater focus: greater clarity about what we're seeking; greater sympathy for those we intercede for, because they are less likely to seem only an abstraction; greater joy; and a greater boost to faith, when we can actually see God's particular answer to our particular prayer.

There's a certain parallel here to the successful business strategy of employing "measurable objectives." In a sense, the more specific and concrete our prayer goals, the more likely we are to see them accomplished. Viewed from this angle, then, more specific prayer appears to have a greater effectiveness, or potential for effectiveness. You might compare it to gardening: we can spend our time scattering seed far and wide, or we can invest our time cultivating a small plot. But the small, cultivated plot is more likely to show the fruit of our labors.

Nevertheless, we must also remember that *someone* needs to be "scattering" the prayer "seed," especially in those places where no one else is doing the job. We all need to be praying some of what we might call the "big picture" prayers.

I think, for example, of a deacon I know who regularly prays at Mass "for all those who have asked for our prayers." Then, he adds, "And for all those who have no one to pray for them." That's a beautiful and powerful intercession. It reflects two realities: God's love for every person, no matter how forgotten by everyone else; and the deacon's desire to love them as God does.

For that reason, whenever people are petitioning Our Lord, I encourage them to include both kinds of prayers, both "deep" and "wide." Each is efficacious in its own way.

— *PT*

Q. Protestants recite a different version of the Our Father from Catholics. Which version — Catholic or Protestant — of the Our Father is correct?

A. The text of this prayer, also known as the Lord's Prayer, is found in Matthew 6:9-13. The Protestant version adds a concluding doxology (a prayer of praise to God): *"For Thine is the kingdom, and the power, and the glory, forever. Amen."*

Some early manuscripts of this Gospel, both in the original Greek languages and in translations, include these words in various forms, but many do not. Most modern translators of the Bible have concluded that the doxology was not in the original text and should appear, if at all, only in marginal notes. In addition, we should note that a parallel passage in the Gospel of Luke (11:2-11) does not include the doxology.

On the other hand, early Catholic liturgies sometimes concluded the Our Father with some kind of doxology. In the early text known as the *Didache*, we find: "For yours are the power and the glory forever."

Another ancient Christian text, the *Apostolic Constitutions*, adds to the beginning of the doxology "the kingdom." The fourth-century Church Father St. John Chrysostom cites the prayer in this form, which is the version now used in the ordinary form of the Roman rite. The Our Father is prayed, then the doxology is spoken by the assembly after the priest prays: "Deliver us, O Lord, from every evil, and grant us peace in our day. Keep us free from sin and protect us from all anxiety, as we await in joyful hope the coming of our Savior, Jesus Christ." (See also *CCC* 2760, 2855.)

For all these reasons, we can't really say that one version is "correct" and the other is "incorrect." Instead, we should view the Our Father, however it's prayed, as one of the common prayers that unite Christians of all kinds. According to one estimate, on Easter Sunday last year, 1 billion Catholic, Orthodox, and Protestant Christians prayed this little prayer in a multitude of languages in churches all around the world.

— *PT*

Q. When should we pray the Apostles' Creed and when should we pray the Nicene Creed? Are they interchangeable?

A. Like all Catholic creeds, the Apostles' and the Nicene provide something of a summary of the faith that we profess. Nevertheless, no brief creed can include every single fundamental Christian belief, and specific historical circumstances shaped which of the fundamentals were included or emphasized in each creed. The result is some variation in content — though, of course, not in doctrine.

Here's an example of a fundamental tenet of faith that is not expressly stated in either creed: the Nicene notes that Christ "rose again in fulfillment of the Scriptures," and that the Holy Spirit "has spoken through the prophets." But it doesn't contain, nor does the Apostles' Creed, an explicit statement of the divine inspiration of Scripture.

Why not? Largely because, in the period when these creeds were developed, there was no serious challenge being raised by heretical factions to the truth that Scripture is divinely inspired (though there were, of course, heretical challenges to the Church's choice of books to be included in the canon — the official list of texts recognized as inspired Scripture).

On the other hand, the Nicene Creed had its origins in the Church's response to an ancient heretical movement (Arianism), which taught that God the Son was a creature made by God the Father, and thus was not fully equal with Him. That's why this creed emphasizes and elaborates the full divinity of Jesus Christ:

> . . . the only Son of God, eternally begotten of the Father; God from God, Light from Light, True God from True God; begotten, not made, one in Being with the Father; through Him [that is, through God the Son] all things were made.

The Apostles' Creed, having developed under different historical circumstances, speaks of Him simply as "Jesus Christ, His [God the Father's] only Son, our Lord."

So which creed, you ask, is best to pray? It depends on the circumstances. The Nicene is normally designated (though not always) as the creed to be recited during Mass. And, of course, during Mass we should be praying together whichever words the Church has carefully chosen for the liturgy.

When we pray the Rosary, on the other hand, the Apostles' Creed is traditionally the one we pray at the beginning. You could, of course, use the Nicene instead if you're praying alone, but if you're praying the Rosary with others, it's better to be praying in unison.

The Apostles' Creed is also the one typically taught to younger children, since it's shorter — and thus, easier to learn.

As for your personal devotions, I would encourage you to vary which creed you use. Since each one has distinctive features, each one has something distinctive to profess and to ponder. What does it mean, for example, when the Nicene Creed says that the Holy Spirit "proceeds from the Father and the Son"? And what does it mean when the Apostles' Creed says that Christ "descended into hell"? That alone is enough to meditate upon for a long time.

— PT

Q. How does someone make a "spiritual communion"?

A. Our Lord wants us to receive Him in His Body, Blood, Soul, and Divinity in Holy Communion, and we should do that as often as possible, making sure that we're properly disposed to receive Him that way. But sometimes, we want to commune with Jesus by receiving the Blessed Sacrament, but circumstances prevent us from doing so.

Perhaps we're homebound. Perhaps we're unable to attend Mass. Perhaps we can attend Mass, but we can't receive Communion because we aren't properly prepared. Perhaps Mass isn't being celebrated when we seek to unite ourselves with Jesus.

Whatever the case, in times when we seek a communion with Our Lord but can't receive Him sacramentally, we can always receive Him spiritually.

Such a "spiritual communion" consists in fervently desiring to receive Jesus in the Eucharist, then embracing Him with love in our hearts as if we had actually received Him in a sacramental Communion. It can be done anywhere: during Mass, during Eucharistic adoration, or anytime outside of church.

In his encyclical letter *Ecclesia de Eucharistia* (*Church of the Eucharist*, 2003), Pope John Paul II had this to say about this praiseworthy spiritual practice:

> In the Eucharist, "unlike any other sacrament, the mystery [of communion] is so perfect that it brings us to the heights of every good thing: Here is the ultimate goal of every human desire, because here we attain God and God joins himself to us in the most perfect union."
>
> Precisely for this reason it is good to *cultivate in our hearts a constant desire for the sacrament of the Eucharist.*
>
> This was the origin of the practice of "spiritual communion," which has happily been established in the Church for centuries and recommended by saints who were masters of the spiritual life.

St. Teresa of Jesus wrote: "When you do not receive communion and you do not attend Mass, you can make a spiritual communion, which is a most beneficial practice; by it the love of God will be greatly impressed on you" (*Way of Perfection*, 35).

How should you pray as you make a spiritual communion? Use your own words, or try this "Act of Spiritual Communion" from the Sacred Apostolic Penitentiary's *Enchiridion of Indulgences*:

My Jesus, I believe that you are in the Blessed Sacrament. I love you above all things, and I long for you in my soul. Since I cannot now receive you sacramentally, come at least spiritually into my heart. As though you have already come, I embrace you and unite myself entirely to you; never permit me to be separated from you. Amen.

The *Enchiridion of Indulgences* also notes that you can gain a partial indulgence by making an act of spiritual communion.

— *PT*

Q. When I gain an indulgence, can I apply it to another person who is still living?

A. We can apply the indulgences we gain to those who are deceased, but not to others who are still living, because they are still in a position to seek indulgences for themselves and to engage in other penitential acts as well.

This instruction was at one time made explicit in the *Code of Canon Law*, in which Canon 930 stated: "No one who gains indulgences can apply them to other living persons." However, the Code was revised in 1983, and in its current form reads instead: "Any member of the faithful can gain partial or plenary indulgences for oneself or apply them to the dead by way of suffrage" (Canon 994).

The newer formulation still implies what the earlier formulation explicitly stated — the category of persons to whom indulgences can be applied comprises oneself and the departed; no others are included.

Even so, we can always pray for those who are still living, have Masses said for their needs and intentions, and offer personal sacrifices to God on their behalf.

— *PT*

Q. Can you pray for someone in hell? Can the sufferings of souls in hell be lessened by our prayers, even though they are eternally damned?

A. Prayers for souls in hell would have no effect on them. Yet you and I cannot know whether any given person is in hell. Even though it may appear to us that a person died while cut off completely from God by his own choices, we should not assume he is in hell. Rather, we should continue to pray for him and trust God to use our prayers as He intends.

The only creatures of God whom we assuredly know to be, or will be, in hell are Satan and his angels. The *Catechism* teaches us that Satan and his angels, using their free will, "radically and irrevocably rejected God and His reign" (*CCC* 392). They cannot be saved because their rejection of God is final.

— *RR*

Q. What is the "Gift of Tears"?

A. The "gift of tears" is one expression of the working of the Holy Spirit. Those who receive this gift insist it is not associated with any emotional upheaval. They do not weep or cry in the ordinary sense of these terms. There is no sobbing or contortion of the face. The tears simply come at times when they are especially aware of the presence of God.

The Eastern tradition has much to say about this gift. A

contemporary Greek Orthodox theologian, Bishop Kallistos Ware, connects this charismatic gift with the gift of tongues:

> When it is genuinely spiritual, "speaking with tongues" seems to represent an act of "letting go," the crucial moment in the breaking down of our sinful self-trust, and its replacement by a willingness to allow God to act with us. In the Orthodox tradition this act of "letting go" more often takes the form of the gift of tears.
>
> — *The Orthodox Way*, St. Vladimir's Seminary Press, 1995, p. 101; emphasis in the original

Eastern writers describe this gift in various ways: the way of tears, the prayer of tears, tears which illuminate, holy sadness. Some regard this gift so important to the spiritual life that they refer to it as "the second baptism." Their point is that while baptism cleanses us from past sin, the gift of tears reflects God's washing away our present sins. Symeon the New Theologian (949-1022) even calls the gift of tears "baptism in the Holy Spirit."

Bishop Ware and other writers on the subject caution that not all tears are a gift of the Spirit. There must be discernment. "Beloved, do not believe every spirit, but test the spirits to see whether they are of God" (1 Jn 4:1).

— *RR*

Q. If Catholics eat meat on Friday, are we supposed to do some other kind of penance? I was told that we could eat meat on Friday only if we made some other sacrifice. True or not true?

A. To answer that question, let's begin with the relevant canons from the 1983 *Code of Canon Law* (emphasis added here and in all citations below):

> 1250: The days and times of penance for the universal Church are *each Friday of the whole year and the season of Lent.*

1251: Abstinence from meat, or from some other food as determined by the Episcopal Conference, *is to be observed on all Fridays, unless a solemnity should fall on a Friday.* Abstinence and fasting are to be observed on Ash Wednesday and Good Friday.

1253: The Episcopal Conference can determine more particular ways in which fasting and abstinence are to be observed. *In place of abstinence or fasting, it can substitute, in whole or in part, other forms of penance,* especially works of charity and exercises of piety.

Pope Paul VI, in the apostolic constitution *Paenitemini* (1966), declared that bishops' conferences may "substitute abstinence and fast wholly or in part with other forms of penitence and especially works of charity and the exercises of piety." He added that "it is up to the bishops — gathered in their episcopal conferences — to establish the norms which, in their pastoral solicitude and prudence, and with the direct knowledge they have of local conditions, they consider the most opportune and efficacious."

Nine months later, the American bishops responded to the new rules by making several modifications in the discipline for Catholics in the U.S. One of these changes referred to abstinence from meat on Fridays outside of Lent. Here's the relevant text from their *Pastoral Statement on Penance and Abstinence* (National Conference of Catholic Bishops, 1966):

22. *Friday itself remains a special day of penitential observance throughout the year,* a time when those who seek perfection will be mindful of their personal sins and the sins of mankind which they are called upon to help expiate in union with Christ Crucified.

23. Friday should be in each week something of what Lent is in the entire year. For this reason we urge all to prepare for that weekly Easter that comes with each Sunday by freely

making of every Friday a day of self-denial and mortification in prayerful remembrance of the passion of Jesus Christ.

24. Among the works of voluntary self-denial and personal penance which we especially commend to our people for the future observance of Friday, *even though we hereby terminate the traditional law of abstinence binding under pain of sin, as the sole prescribed means of observing Friday, we give first place to abstinence from flesh meat.* We do so in the hope that the Catholic community will *ordinarily continue to abstain from meat by free choice* as formerly we did in obedience to Church law. Our expectation is based on the following considerations:

a. We shall thus freely and out of love for Christ Crucified show our solidarity with the generations of believers to whom this practice frequently became, especially in times of persecution and of great poverty, no mean evidence of fidelity to Christ and His Church.

b. We shall thus also remind ourselves that as Christians, although immersed in the world and sharing its life, we must preserve a saving and necessary difference from the spirit of the world. Our deliberate, personal abstinence from meat, more especially because no longer required by law, will be an outward sign of inward spiritual values that we cherish.

— www.usccb.org/lent/2007/Penance_and_Abstinence.pdf

In 1983, the National Conference of Catholic Bishops issued the pastoral letter *The Challenge of Peace: God's Promise and Our Response*. In it, they reaffirmed the normal penitential status of Fridays throughout the year:

As a tangible sign of our need and desire to do penance we, for the cause of peace, commit ourselves to fast and abstinence on each Friday of the year. *We call upon our people voluntarily to do penance on Friday by eating less food and by abstaining from meat.* This return to a traditional practice of penance, once well observed in the U.S. Church, should be accompanied by works of charity and service toward our neighbors. *Every Friday should be a day significantly devoted to prayer, penance, and almsgiving for peace.*

— N. 298

It seems to me abundantly clear from all these documents that observing the penitential nature of Fridays throughout the year remains an essential part of Catholic discipline, in the U.S. as elsewhere, and that abstinence from meat on those days is still the preferred form of that discipline. Nothing in these statements even remotely suggests that Catholics who choose not to abstain from meat on Fridays are not obliged to substitute some other penance instead.

— *PT*

Q. Is our tithe supposed to be on the amount we get taxed on or the amount we bring home? Also, is that 10 percent amount that we tithe supposed to go entirely to the Church, or can it be divvied up between the Church, the poor box, and any charitable organizations — or are those in addition to our obligated giving?

A. The Church holds as one of her precepts (commandments): "You shall help to provide for the needs of the Church." According to the *Catechism of the Catholic Church*, this means that "the faithful are obliged to assist with the material needs of the Church, each according to his own ability" (*CCC* 2043).

Beyond this general obligation, the Church as a whole formally offers no detailed rules. A few American bishops have published guidelines for their particular dioceses, suggesting that a portion go to the local parish, a portion to the diocese, and a portion to charitable causes.

Some would argue that the Old Testament commandments to give a tithe (the literal meaning of "tithe" is 10 percent) still hold for God's people today. (See, for example, Malachi 3:8-10, where God tells His people through the prophet Malachi that they are "robbing" Him by failing to give Him a tithe.) Nevertheless, the Church has concluded that the principle of generous giving, rather than the exact fraction, has continued under the New Covenant.

We should keep in mind that in many cases where the Law under the Old Covenant gave way to a new obligation for God's people, the new obligation was *more* demanding than the old, not less. (See, for example, Mt 5:21-48.)

We should also recall that when Jesus reprimanded the hypocritical scribes and Pharisees for making tithes even of their herbs while neglecting "weightier matters," He didn't tell them that the tithe was of no account; He said, "These you should have done, without neglecting the others" (Mt 23:23). He also spoke approvingly of the impoverished widow who gave God her last two small coins (see Lk 21:2).

As an old Bible teacher I once knew used to say, "You can't outgive God." We should also keep in mind Our Lord's words: "Where your treasure is, there also will your heart be" (Mt 6:21). A Christian's faithfulness in giving to God, or failing to do so, is a matter of great importance; it's one indicator of spiritual health.

— *PT*

Q. Why does the Church have the right to make laws (the precepts of the Church)? Are they as binding as the Ten Commandments? If so, why?

A. The Church has the right, power, and obligation to make laws, because not only is the Church the Mystical Body of Christ, it is also a visible society of persons, and a society must have laws by which it is organized. Moreover, Our Lord said to St. Peter:

> "I will give you the keys to the kingdom of heaven, and whatever you bind on earth shall be bound in heaven; and whatever you loose on earth shall be loosed in heaven."

— Mt 16:19

All valid ecclesiastical laws must be consistent with the natural law, and as such, would be as binding as the Ten Commandments, all other things being equal.

— *FH*

Q. Where does the term "Holy See" come from and what does it mean?

A. The "Holy See" refers to the pope and his court. The English word *see* (which, of course, has a different origin from its homograph *see*, "to perceive with the eye") comes from an Old French word, which itself comes from the Latin *sedes*, meaning "seat." This term has its origin in the episcopal throne, or bishop's chair (the *cathedra*), set up in his cathedral — a symbol of his ecclesiastical authority.

Technically, the *see* of a bishop is his *charge*: his authority, responsibility, and jurisdiction. More broadly, the term "see" has come to refer to the functions of government, the whole administration, which attach to the bishop's charge. We can speak, then, of the archepiscopal See of New York, the episcopal See of Savannah, and the Holy See.

We should note that the terms *see* and *diocese* are not equivalent. The *see* of a bishop differs from his *diocese* in that the latter refers specifically to the territorial aspect of his see — the geographic extent of his authority, responsibility, and jurisdiction.

— *PT*

Q. Is there a canonical process for removing a pope?

A. No, there is not. The Roman pontiff, "by virtue of his office, has supreme, full, immediate and universal ordinary power in the Church, and he can always freely exercise this power" (Canon 331). He cannot be removed, although the law of the Church does provide for the possibility of his resignation (see Canon 332.2). For instance, Pope St. Celestine V resigned in 1294 after five months in office. Pope Gregory XII (1406-1415) resigned to end the Papal Schism when three men claimed to be the true pope: Pope Gregory, Avignon Pope Benedict XII, and Antipope John XXIII.

— *FH*

Q. What is the bishop's "crosier"?

A. The bishop's *crosier* is a staff, made of either metal or wood, with a curved crook at its top. It recalls the staff used by ancient shepherds to tend their flocks. Remember how King David, who was once a shepherd himself, says in Psalm 23 that the Lord is his caring "shepherd" (v. 1), whose "rod" and "staff" comfort him (v. 4)?

The crosier reminds both bishops and their flocks that he stands among them representing Christ, the "Good Shepherd," who "lays down His life for His sheep" (Jn 10:11).

This staff is held by the bishop when in procession; during the proclamation of the Gospel and the homily; when receiving religious vows and promises or a profession of faith; and when bestowing a blessing, except when the blessing includes the laying on of hands.

Your question reminds me of an incident some years ago, when Pope John Paul II was lying in state at the Vatican before his funeral. A news story from the *International Herald Tribune*, written by a reporter for *The New York Times*, declared that "tucked under his left arm was the silver staff, called the crow's ear, that he had carried in public."

They meant to say, of course, the *crosier*. The remarkable fact that neither the reporter assigned to this major story at this major newspaper, nor even the many editors and proofreaders who reviewed it, had a clue that "crow's ear" was an error, tells us volumes about how ignorant the secular press can be about Catholic matters.

— *PT*

Q. When is it the duty of the local bishop to excommunicate someone from the Church?

A. First, let's clarify some concepts. The local bishop does not excommunicate persons; canon law does. For a person to be excommunicated, first, the law must be on the books; then, he has to know about it; and, finally, he has to break it. In such a case, he is either automatically excommunicated (*latae sententiae*) or excommunicated by the decree of the bishop or declaration of the sentence by the competent ecclesiastical tribunal (*ferendae sententiae*).

In this second case, the bishop or tribunal merely determines from the facts of the case that the law was indeed broken and the person in question is guilty. So, perhaps your question should be: "When should the local bishop inform someone that he or she has been excommunicated?" But first let's take a look at the very notion of this penalty.

Excommunication is the most serious penalty that can be imposed upon a member of the Church. Those who have been excommunicated cannot receive or celebrate the sacraments until they have been forgiven through sacramental absolution and a competent authority has lifted the penalty. Since the Church is in the business of saving souls, the penal remedy of excommunication seeks to give the sinner a powerful wake-up call to conversion.

The most serious "crimes" trigger automatic excommunication reserved to the Holy See: desecration of the Holy Eucharist; use of physical force against the pope; absolution of an accomplice in a crime against the Sixth Commandment; consecration of a bishop without the approval of the Holy See; and breaking the seal of the confessional.

But other crimes also bring automatic excommunication, although they can be forgiven and the penalty can be lifted locally. Canon law lists four of these: apostasy, heresy, schism, and abortion.

The bishop should make sure that the penalty of excommunication is applied according to the norms of canon law, which above all seeks to protect the good of the Church and the conversion of the person who committed a crime. With respect to automatic excommunication (*latae sententiae*), the bishop has a great deal of discretion as to how, when, and whom he should inform about such matters. But when applying such penalties, he must always keep two goals in mind: first, that there be clarity about the faith and morals taught by the Church; and, second, that such measures be a spiritual help to the person in question.

— *FH*

Q. Are public notifications prohibiting Catholic politicians from receiving Communion if they support abortion the same as excommunication?

A. No, public notification prohibiting Catholic politicians from receiving the Holy Eucharist if they support abortion or euthanasia is not an excommunication, but the application of a general precept of the Church. Canon 915 states, "Those who . . . obstinately [persevere] in manifest grave sin are not to be admitted to Holy Communion."

Archbishop Raymond Burke's notification read:

A Catholic legislator who supports procured abortion or euthanasia, after knowing the teaching of the Church, commits a manifestly grave sin which is a cause of most serious scandal to others.

We should be united in praying for bishops everywhere that God may give them the grace, wisdom, and strength to carry out their ministry in an effective way.

— *FH*

Q. What makes a particular church a cathedral?

A. Our English word *cathedral* comes from a Latin term, which ultimately comes from the Greek word *kathédra*, meaning "chair." Since ancient times, the chair has served as a symbol of spiritual teaching authority.

A cathedral is thus the church containing the chair of the bishop, and it serves as the central church of the diocese over which he has jurisdiction. The bishop is pastor of the cathedral, but he has so many additional responsibilities for the diocese that he typically appoints a *rector*, that is, a priest who assumes pastoral duties in the cathedral parish on his behalf.

Usually, the cathedral is the site of the principal liturgical activities of the bishop and his diocese. Here, the bishop is consecrated and enthroned upon his *cathedra*; here, diocesan synods are usually held. In his cathedral, the bishop most properly ordains, confirms, blesses holy oils, celebrates the liturgies of the Sacred Triduum, and presides at Pontifical Masses. Bishops are often buried in a cathedral crypt.

The cathedral must be located within the diocese it serves, usually in the see city where the bishop exercises his authority. Occasionally, for various historical or geographic reasons, a diocese may have two *co-cathedrals*, usually in different cities but sometimes in the same city. A *pro-cathedral* is one used by the bishop as his cathedral until a more suitable church can be built.

— *PT*

Q. What's a monsignor?

A. The address *monsignor* (from the Italian "my lord") has been used generally to refer to Church dignitaries of various sorts, such as bishops, higher officials of the Church administration in Rome, abbots and other major superiors of religious orders, and others.

However, you are probably referring to those who are addressed as *monsignor* because they have received one of several honorary ranks conferred by the pope on a priest, usually at the request of his bishop, in recognition of outstanding service to the Church. From lowest to highest rank, they may be designated as a "Chaplain to His Holiness," "Prelate of Honor," or "Protonotary Apostolic."

— *PT*

Q. What is the difference between a monk and a friar?

A. Though the term *monk* is commonly used to designate all male religious, it more properly refers to a member of a community of men that leads a more or less contemplative life apart from the world, under vows of poverty, chastity, and obedience, according to a formal rule. Monks tend to remain living in one place, and they chant in choir the Divine Office of daily prayer.

The English word *monk* comes ultimately from the Greek *monos*, meaning "solitary" or "alone." Some examples of monastic communities would be the Benedictines, the Cistercians, and the Carthusians.

Friars (literally, "brothers") are also male religious who live in community under a formal rule; like monks, they pray the Divine Office in choir. But they aren't properly called "monks" because their work of preaching, going out among those in the world, soliciting alms, and moving from place to place aren't consistent with the monastic ideal.

While the vow of poverty for monks allows the community

to own property corporately, originally the friars were allowed neither individual nor corporate ownership of property; they had no fixed revenues to live on and relied totally on the voluntary offerings of the faithful. This restriction (which was eventually modified) meant that begging for alms was an important part of their activity; that's why they also came to be called *mendicants* (literally, "beggars"). Some examples of friars would be the Dominicans, the Franciscans, and the Augustinians.

Under the entry for "friar," *A Catholic Dictionary* (ed., Donald Attwater; 3rd ed., Macmillan, 1958) provides this useful comparison:

> "Friar" is not synonymous with "monk"; they are as different as artillery from infantry; the life of a monk is normally passed within the walls of his monastery; a friar has his headquarters in a friary but his work is of the active ministry and may take him to all parts of the earth; a friar is a member of a highly organized, widespread body with a central authority to which he is professed; a monk's allegiance is to the abbot of an autonomous individual monastery.

We should also note that *clerks regular* form a third class of male religious. Though they, too, are bodies of men in the Church bound by solemn religious vows and living in a religious community under a rule, they're engaged primarily in the active work of priestly ministry. Unlike the monks and mendicants, they aren't expected to pray the Daily Office in choir. The Jesuits, the Theatines, and the Barnabites are three examples of clerks regular.

— PT

Q. How does a person properly dispose of old blessed Bibles?

A. As far as I can determine, the Church has not mandated a procedure for disposing of old Bibles. If they are still in usable condition, why not donate them to a Catholic mission or other organization that could make good use of them? If the Bibles in question are falling apart or otherwise dilapidated, however, since they've been blessed, I'd encourage you to follow the Catholic tradition that respectfully disposes of blessed religious items by burning or burying. When you do that, you might also say a prayer thanking God for giving us the Scripture and asking Him to grant His grace to all who have used these copies of it.

— *FH*

Q. Is it customary to pay a regular fee or honorarium to a spiritual director?

A. It is not usual to pay for spiritual direction, but if your spiritual director has no other way to support him or herself, then I suppose it would be appropriate. After all, Our Lord said that the "laborer deserves his pay" (Mt 10:10). Nevertheless, the tradition of the Church in this matter is based on Our Lord's instructions to the apostles: "You received without pay, give without pay" (Mt 10:8).

— *FH*

Q. Is Halloween a pagan or a Christian holiday?

A. In terms of its origins, Halloween is both pagan and Christian. In terms of its practice, that depends on who's celebrating!

Before the coming of the Christian faith to Celtic lands (the British Isles and Brittany), a pagan feast that seems to have been associated with the harvest and New Year's Eve on the Celtic calendar took place on the night of October 31. In the Druid religion (practiced by the Celts), the night of October 31 was considered a time when the lord of death, named Samhain, allowed the souls of the dead to roam. (Some scholars, we should note, have disputed some specifics of these historical claims.)

After the Christian faith had spread among Celtic peoples, that same night eventually came to be observed in the Church calendar as the eve of All Saints' Day, which honors all the Christian saints in heaven, both known and unknown. In fact, the name "Halloween" is a contraction of "All Hallows' Evening." "Hallows" means "holy ones," or saints.

As for its current practice, whether the holiday is Christian or pagan depends largely on whether the emphasis is on the demonic and macabre, or on the memory of those who reign with Our Lord now in heaven. Obviously, the secular culture, lacking faith, emphasizes the former. But many Christians, Catholic and otherwise, have found ways to observe the day that are both entertaining and spiritually focused.

— PT

Q. What is the proper way to ship cremated remains?

A. First of all, Canon 1176.3 states:

The Church earnestly recommends that the pious custom of burial be retained; but it does not forbid cremation, unless this is chosen for reasons which are contrary to Christian teaching.

The Church stipulates only that the cremated remains be treated with respect. If you are planning on shipping the remains, I would suggest that a trusted person be charged with carrying the cremated remains with him on the plane, rather than ship them "air freight." Piety and common sense suggest that disposition, although Church law has no such regulations.

In most places in our country, the cremated remains may not be shipped unless accompanied by three official documents: the death certificate from the medical doctor verified by the coroner; the permit from the registrar, who was notified by the coroner, allowing cremation; and the certificate from the crematorium.

— FH

Q. Has the Church lifted its condemnation of the Masons? I heard a radio broadcast about the recent discovery of a document related to the medieval trial of the Templars, which vindicates them.

A. Catholics are still forbidden to be Masons. But the Templars and the Masons aren't the same thing.

The military order of the Poor Knights of Christ and of the Temple of Solomon (commonly known as the Templars) was founded in Jerusalem in 1118 to protect Christians in the Holy Land. The order became widespread, powerful, and wealthy, but it eventually fell into disfavor with the powerful King Philip IV of France (1268-1314). Apparently, Philip either wanted their money or wanted to cancel the debts he owed the order. So he arrested members of the Knights and tortured them until he extracted confessions of heresy and sexual immorality.

In 1308, however, Pope Clement V decided to save the order — as recorded by the document to which you refer, the "Parchment of Chinon." It was recently reviewed by an official at the Vatican Secret Archives, who discovered that it contained information not recognized before because of an error in archiving.

The parchment reproduces the documentation of the papal hearings convened after Philip IV arrested and tortured the Templars. It reveals that the cardinals acting as judges in the trial finally concluded that Templar members had indeed been guilty of moral abuses, but not of heresy. Only in that limited sense were they "exonerated."

This was during the time of the so-called "Avignon Papacy," when the popes resided in Avignon, France, and as a result were often dominated by the French royalty. King Philip pressured the pope to suppress the Templars, which the latter finally did in 1312. They were never reinstated by any of Clement's successors, so the group no longer exists as an approved order in the service of the Church.

(As a side note, in 2007, the Holy See publicly declared as false a letter allegedly written by Vatican Secretary of State Cardinal Angelo Sodano that said Rome had recognized a new order of Knights Templar. The false document had circulated in Germany for months, and Rome had received numerous inquiries about it.)

Today, there may be associations of "Templars" that are, in fact, Masonic in nature and origin. But these Masonic groups actually have nothing at all to do with the venerable history of the original Knights Templar. They have simply appropriated some of the Knights' symbols and rituals for their own purposes.

Much has been written about Freemasonry and the Catholic Church in recent years, and Catholics are still forbidden to belong to any Masonic group because the principles of Masonry are incompatible with the Catholic faith.

According to the 1917 *Code of Canon Law*, a Catholic incurred the penalty of automatic excommunication if he joined the Masons (see Canon 2335, *CIC* 1917). While Masonic and Templar groups are not *specifically* mentioned in the current *Code of Canon Law* (1983), membership in such groups is prohibited by virtue of Canon 1374:

> A person who joins an association which plots against the Church is to be punished with a just penalty; one who promotes or takes office in such an association is to be punished with an interdict.

Since Masonry is not specifically mentioned in the 1983 Code, a question was posed to the Sacred Congregation for the Doctrine of the Faith. Its response, signed by then-prefect Cardinal Joseph Ratzinger (now Pope Benedict XVI) and specifically approved by the reigning Roman Pontiff, John Paul II, stated:

> Therefore the Church's negative judgment in regard to Masonic associations remains unchanged since their principles have always been considered irreconcilable with the doctrine of the Church and therefore membership in them remains forbidden. The faithful who enroll in Masonic

associations are in a state of grave sin and may not receive Holy Communion.

— CDF, *Quaesitum Est*, November 26, 1983

The U.S. bishops returned to this topic in 1985 and added this helpful clarification about the different ways Masonry was treated in the 1917 Code (penalty of excommunication) and the 1983 Code (gravely immoral, but no specific canonical penalty):

What is at stake is the distinction between penal law and morality. There is a difference between the two. Not everything that is immoral is penalized in the Church. Nor can one conclude from the fact that penal law does not cover some sin or that it is removed from it (or changed), that it is permissible to commit it.

A clear example of this is abortion. Even if the excommunication were removed from abortion, it would still be wrong. Similarly, even if the excommunication was removed from joining an organization that plotted against the Church, it would still be wrong to join such an organization.

— Cardinal Bernard Law, Letter of April 19, 1985,
to U.S. Bishops Concerning Masonry

— *PT*

Q. Should Reiki practitioners be allowed at Catholic hospitals? Is Reiki a New Age or even occult practice?

A. Unfortunately, all too often Catholic hospitals have promoted Reiki and other questionable practices. In 2009, the United States Conference of Catholic Bishops (USCCB) released a statement clarifying that Reiki has no place in Catholic medical care. It's called *Guidelines for Evaluating Reiki as an Alternative Therapy*.

A few of the document's most important insights:

Reiki is a technique of healing that was invented in Japan in the late 1800s by Mikao Usui, who was studying Buddhist texts. According to Reiki teaching, illness is caused by some kind of disruption or imbalance in one's "life energy." A Reiki practitioner effects healing by placing his or her hands in certain positions on the patient's body in order to facilitate the flow of Reiki, the "universal life energy," from the Reiki practitioner to the patient. There are numerous designated hand positions for addressing different problems. Reiki proponents assert that the practitioner is not the source of the healing energy, but merely a channel for it. To become a Reiki practitioner, one must receive an "initiation" or "attunement" from a Reiki Master. This ceremony makes one "attuned" to the "universal life energy" and enables one to serve as a conduit for it. There are said to be three different levels of attunement (some teach that there are four). At the higher levels, one can allegedly channel Reiki energy and effect healings at a distance, without physical contact.

Though Reiki proponents often claim that it is not a religion, it has several aspects of a religion: "spiritual healing," "sacred ceremonies," references to a God or Goddess or "divine consciousness," "universal life energy," and more. These aspects are rooted in Eastern religions rather than the Christian faith. So is the notion that healing "energy," rather than a gift of divine grace bestowed by God at His discretion, is in fact capable of being manipulated and used by the practitioner, who has been trained in techniques to do so.

The non-Christian religious elements of the practice are not the only problem with Reiki. The document notes that its claim to "universal life energy" and the ability to manipulate it have not been accepted by modern medical science. Reiki lacks scientific credibility and tends toward superstition.

The document concludes:

Reiki finds no support either in the findings of natural science or in Christian belief. For a Catholic to believe in Reiki presents insoluble problems.... Since Reiki therapy is not compatible with either Christian teaching or scientific evidence, it would be inappropriate for Catholic institutions, such as Catholic health care facilities and retreat centers, or persons representing the Church, such as Catholic chaplains, to promote or provide support for Reiki therapy.

— NN. 10, 12

— *PT*

Q. What is "Easter laughter"?

A. "Easter laughter," known in Latin as *Risus Paschalis*, is the custom of including jokes or funny stories in Easter homilies, then drawing spiritual lessons from them. The rationale for the tradition is that Easter was Our Lord's great cosmic "joke" on the devil, giving Him the last laugh. Just when Satan thought he'd triumphed over the Son of God, the tables were turned, and the enemy of our souls discovered that God had outwitted him, using him to carry out the great plan of redemption for the fallen human race.

Telling a joke on Easter, then, is offering a token of the Christian's scorn for the devil's folly.

The custom was once common in gatherings held on Easter afternoon or evening throughout Central Europe. Similar traditions developed in the East, with humorous celebrations on Easter Monday.

Some scholars have suggested that the "Easter laughter" custom originated in Bavaria in the fifteenth century, but other sources insist that post-Easter celebrations and festivals actually originated with the early Greek Christians. In any case, in Bavaria, the practice apparently evolved over time into displays of irreverence that eventually led to its prohibition in the seventeenth century by Pope Clement X (1670-1676), and in the eighteenth century by Elector Maximilian III of Bavaria and the bishops of Bavaria.

— *PT*

Q. What should I tell my children about Santa Claus? We have arguments in my extended family every year about the matter.

A. It's a perennial debate among Christians: is Santa Claus a bit of harmless fun? Or is the tale actually a lie that turns kids' attention away from Jesus?

Why not just tell children the truth? Tell them the story of the real, historical St. Nicholas — a man whose life pointed beautifully to Jesus. If we share with them the story of the real St. Nicholas, we won't be turning their attention away from Jesus. Instead, we'll be showing them how the Child of the manger can shine, even now, through a heart that's devoted to Him.

Born in Asia Minor more than sixteen centuries ago, Nicholas was a bishop who gave his life to serve others. He worked miracles and brought many people to faith in Christ. He also shared his wealth with the poor and took special care of children. We don't know much more for sure than that, though legends abound. But this much is certain: St. Nicholas shone so brightly with the love of Jesus that Christians came to honor him all over the world.

Over the years, some honored him by dressing up like him and giving children gifts. As his fame spread across many countries, his costume and his name took many forms. The Dutch called him "Santa Claus" and introduced him to America. In our country, the red suit, sleigh, and reindeer were added to his portrait.

Whatever we may think of these more recent notions of St. Nicholas, they shouldn't keep us from telling our children the truth about a great servant of God.

— *PT*

6.

Questions about Catholic History

Q. How did the Evangelists — St. Matthew, St. Mark, St. Luke, and St. John — die?

A. St. Matthew was, of course, one of the twelve apostles. According to ancient tradition, he preached in the East and died as a martyr for the Faith. One tradition says he died in Ethiopia; another says it was in Persia (present-day Iran).

St. Mark was, according to ancient tradition, a companion of St. Peter in Rome and wrote his Gospel from that apostle's perspective. One tradition also reports that he died a martyr's death in Alexandria, Egypt, after having preached the Gospel there.

St. Luke was one of St. Paul's traveling companions and wrote his Gospel under the influence of that apostle. He is believed to have died at Boeotia, a region of Greece, at the age of eighty-four.

St. John had the responsibility (given to him by Jesus) of caring for Our Lady after Our Lord's death. Although traditionally the Church has not commemorated him as a martyr (the only apostle so celebrated), some earlier traditions (perhaps derived from the witness of the second-century bishop Papias of Hierapolis) suggest that he, too, was martyred.

— PT

Q. Are the Fathers of the Church and the Doctors of the Church the same people?

A. The two categories overlap, but they are not the same.

Those designated as *Fathers* of the Church are significant teachers from the early centuries of the Church whose writings on

Christian doctrine and morals are considered to have great weight and to be worthy of great respect (though the teaching of any particular Father is obviously not infallible). These men were also characterized by notable holiness of life.

Why call them "fathers"? In the New Testament, the term "father" is sometimes used to refer to someone who teaches the Faith by word and by example (see, for example, 1 Cor 4:15-16). The first teachers of the Catholic faith were collectively spoken of as "the Fathers" (see 2 Pet 3:4). Those now designated as the Church Fathers played a critical role in nourishing the infant Church through their teaching and personal holiness.

Most of those on the list are universally recognized as belonging there: St. Ignatius of Antioch, St. Gregory of Nyssa, St. Augustine, and St. John Chrysostom, to name just a few. But scholars still debate about whether a few particular names should be included on the list.

Why the debate? In part, because scholars disagree about how late in Church history the designation should be allowed: Seventh century? Twelfth? Later? They also argue over whether we should include influential ancient teachers, such as Origen, who taught much that is praiseworthy but also taught some ideas that the Church has rejected; as well as those who ultimately ended up in schism, such as Tertullian.

As for the *Doctors* of the Church, the term comes from the Latin word *doctor*, which literally means "teacher." It's related to our English word *doctrine*, literally, "teaching." This is why college professors often have Ph.D.s — an abbreviation for "Doctor" (Teacher) of Philosophy."

Unlike the case with Fathers of the Church, the Church maintains an official list of those she recognizes as Doctors of the Church. These men and women are noted for the greatness of their spiritual or theological learning and their holiness of life. There are currently 33 saints (including four women) who are formally recognized in this way.

All the Doctors of the Church are recognized as saints as well, and they come from all periods of Church history, including modern times. (For example, St. Thérèse of Lisieux lived in the nineteenth century.)

Not surprisingly, some of the great teachers of the Faith from the early centuries are both Doctors and Fathers of the Church (St. Jerome, St. Basil the Great, St. Ambrose, St. Gregory the Great, and others). Some people expect that Pope John Paul II may be added to the list of Doctors as well.

— PT

Q. What is the *Didache*?

A. Several books were highly regarded in parts of the early Church — so much so that some local churches read from them publicly in Mass as if they were Scripture — yet were not included in the final biblical canon by the universal Church. Among these would be such books as the *Didache* (or *Teaching of the Twelve Apostles*), the *Epistle of Clement,* the *Shepherd of Hermas*, the *Wisdom of Solomon,* the *Acts of Peter*, the *Acts of Paul*, the *Apocalypse of Peter,* the *Epistle of Barnabas*, and the *Gospel of the Hebrews*.

Some of these books make for more edifying reading than others.

For example, the *Didache*, written perhaps as early as A.D. 60, gives us a fascinating glimpse into life in the churches of the first generation of Christians. The *Epistle of Clement* (also known as "1 Clement") is full of godly instructions for Christian life from Pope St. Clement I, written perhaps as early as c. A.D. 90 by a man who had known St. Peter and other apostles. (Both of these books were composed before the last of the books in the New Testament canon.)

On the other hand, the *Acts of Peter* (probably dating from a century after the books just named) provides entertaining tales of St. Peter which can sometimes stretch our sense of credulity. In one anecdote, for example, the book claims that St. Peter spoke to

a smoked tuna hanging in a window and raised it back to life, so
that it swam around in a pond and ate bread crumbs! With God
all things are possible, of course, but it may be that the Church
rejected this book from the canon because of such stories as these.

The *Apocalypse of Peter* claims to report what Jesus showed
Peter about the end of the world and the torments of hell. In fact,
it's the earliest of the so-called Christian "tours of hell" books
that purport to describe the tortures of the damned in detail.
(The most famous book in this genre is Dante's *Inferno*.) The
Church most likely rejected this "Apocalypse" because Church
leaders came to realize that it was not, in fact, written by St. Peter
but was composed much later. Nevertheless, it exerted tremen-
dous influence among Christians over the notions of hell and the
end of the world that later developed.

Other books from this period and later, such as the so-called
Gospel of Thomas and *Gospel of Mary*, were influenced by the heresy called Gnosticism. These were not read as Scripture in orthodox churches and never seem to have been seriously considered
for the canon by Church authorities. They may make for interesting reading, but they should not be viewed as reliable sources of
Catholic teaching or early Christian history.

— PT

Q. Who were the Gnostics?

A. Answering this question would require an entire book!
But, in brief, the Gnostics were proponents of a religious heresy
that came into prominence in the Church's second century, and
some traces of this heresy still appear from time to time.

Many (though not all) Gnostics believed in two gods at war
with each other. The god of this world was an evil god, whom
they identified with the god of the Old Testament. Opposed to
the evil god was a higher god, whom Jesus Christ revealed. They
believed this world had been created by evil powers who sought

to keep human souls imprisoned in physical bodies, which were themselves evil.

Further, they believed that salvation (that is, escape from this evil world) came through esoteric knowledge (Greek *gnosis*) imparted to a select few. Gnostic systems of thought, especially those of Valentinus and Basilides, were filled with fanciful speculation about the cosmos.

— PT

Q. As a Catholic am I allowed to read the Gnostic gospels? I've heard about the Gospel of Mary Magdalene, the Gospel of Philip, the Gospel of Thomas, the Gospel of Peter, and the Gospel of Bartholomew.

A. These and other "gospels" are part of a large body of literature — so-called gospels, acts, epistles, and so on — that the Church rejected because they are filled with error. The Church understandably does not give publicity to any heretical writings, but you are certainly free to read them.

Some are literally fantastic; some are even amusing. Many claim to give detailed information about Jesus' infancy, childhood, and youth. Scholars differ as to which ones are strictly Gnostic writings.

Sometimes, playmates decide to ostracize one of their members, often for no good reason. One "gospel" relates that this happened to Jesus. His playmates ran from Him, hid in a cellar, and told their mothers not to tell Jesus where they were. In looking for his playmates, Jesus heard a noise in the cellar and asked one of the mothers what caused the noise. She assured Him it was only a bunch of goats there. Jesus said, "Let the goats come forth," and thereby turned the children into goats. When the mothers (naturally) pleaded for the restoration of their children, Jesus turned them back into human form.

The same book tells a fantastic story about how young Jesus

made clay figures of birds one day. At Jesus' command, they turned into real birds who ate, drank, and flew away.

The *Pseudo-Gospel of Matthew* claims to report on the Holy Family's flight into Egypt. On the third day of that journey, Mary saw a palm tree and asked for some of its fruit. Joseph objected that the tree was far too high to climb. Thereupon, the infant Jesus — from His mother's lap — commanded the tree to bend down and give its fruit to His mother. (This event was supposed to have taken place only a few days after Jesus' birth.) The tree obeyed. After Mary had picked the fruit, the infant Jesus bade the tree rise to its upright position, and again it obeyed.

That same "gospel" gives several examples of how Jesus, as a little boy, dealt with a few of the inevitable neighborhood bullies. When they jumped on Him, or disturbed Him at play, He made them fall down dead. After remonstration by their parents or by St. Joseph, He brought them back to life. Presumably, they gave Him no further trouble.

— *RR*

Q. Has the Catholic Church always been opposed to abortion?

A. The short answer is yes.

The *Catechism of the Catholic Church* summarizes the matter:

Since the first century the Church has affirmed the moral evil of every procured abortion. This teaching has not changed and remains unchangeable. Direct abortion, that is to say, abortion willed either as an end or a means, is gravely contrary to the moral law.

— *CCC* 2271

From the earliest times, Christians have firmly rejected abortion and infanticide. Note, for example, the ancient books known as the *Didache* and the *Epistle of Barnabas*. In the first and second centuries, these were two of the most widely used documents for Christian teaching and practice, after the New Testament. Both texts explicitly condemned abortion and infanticide. Early Church councils did the same.

Admittedly, until modern times little was known about human embryology. Such limited knowledge caused some theologians of the past to speculate about when, in the womb, the individual soul was created by God and joined to the body. But even those who (mistakenly) thought that such "ensoulment" took place sometime after conception nevertheless affirmed that abortion at any stage is a grave sin.

— PT

Q. Was there really a St. Valentine? How did St. Valentine's Day come to be associated with romance?

A. Yes, there really was a St. Valentine — in fact, there were three of them, and a Pope Valentine as well.

At least three St. Valentines who were martyrs are associated with February 14 in the ancient martyrologies. All we know about one of them is that he was put to death with a number of companions in Africa. A second one was a priest of Rome and the third was a bishop of Interamna (modern Terni, Italy).

Apparently these latter two were both martyred in the second half of the third century and were buried (at separate locations) on the Flaminian Way, a road that leads into Rome. In the twelfth century, what had been known in ancient times as the Flaminian Gate of Rome was called the Gate of St. Valentine.

It's now called the Porta del Popolo, or "Gate of the People." That name seems to have come from a church in the immediate neighborhood that was dedicated to the saint. Some *Acta* ("Acts") of these two saints have been preserved, but the texts are of a relatively late date and are historically unreliable.

Pope Valentine, by the way, was by all accounts a devout

pontiff who died in 827 after reigning on St. Peter's throne only a few weeks.

As for the connection with romance, in medieval England and France there was a common belief that on February 14, birds began to pair. The fourteenth-century English poet Chaucer, for example, once wrote of "St. Valentine's Day, when every bird comes there to choose his mate." (I've modernized the language and spelling here.) The day came to be dedicated to lovers and viewed as the proper occasion for writing love letters and sending romantic tokens of affection. People who engaged in this custom called each other their "Valentines."

— PT

Q. When did the Holy Host replace the bread and wine? Jesus used bread and wine. Why did the Church change it?

A. The Church has never changed from using bread and wine as Jesus did. The Host is bread before it is consecrated to become Our Lord's Body, even though it more closely resembles what has come in our time to be called a "wafer." This bread is made simply of wheat flour and natural water that has been mixed and baked.

The first Eucharist, at which Our Lord Jesus presided, was a Passover meal. This means the bread He used was unleavened — that is, flat, without yeast to make it rise, like the matzoh used by observant Jews during Passover even today.

Given this precedent, Christians in the West have continued to use unleavened bread, though it has taken on various shapes, sizes, and thicknesses throughout the Church's history. Some historical evidence suggests that as early as the sixth century, hosts were being used that were as small and thin as they are now.

In the East, on the other hand, Christians have tended to use leavened bread, which in that regard looks more like the common bread we eat today.

As for wine: the priest does, in fact, still consecrate wine and consume Our Lord's precious Blood at every Mass, even at those times when the cup is not shared with the others assembled. So the Church continues, as she always has, to consecrate bread and wine for the Eucharist.

— RR

Q. Do pretzels really have their origin in medieval Lenten practices?

A. Yes, according to tradition, that's correct. In earlier times, Lenten abstinence laws were much stricter than they are now. Throughout the forty days — not just on Fridays (but not on Sundays) — Catholics abstained from eating not only meat but also eggs and dairy products. Only one meal was taken a day, usually toward evening, though eventually the meal was moved up to 3:00 p.m., or even noon.

After the meal became established at the earlier time of day, a collation (small snack) came to be allowed in the evening. People needed some kind of light food that fit the abstinence rules, and pretzels filled the bill.

Traditions vary about the exact origins of the snack. One popular story says that a young monk in the early seventh century in Italy was preparing a special Lenten bread made of water, flour, and salt. (No eggs, milk, or lard could be used as ingredients). To remind the other monks that Lent was a time of prayer, he rolled the dough in strips and twisted each strip in the distinctive pretzel shape we know today. This design reflected what was then a popular prayer posture of crossing the arms upon the chest.

The dough was baked to become a soft bread like the large soft pretzels we sometimes enjoy today. In time, the smaller, hard-baked variety was developed as well (not to mention pretzel sticks).

And the origin of the name? One tradition says it comes from the Latin word *bracellae*, meaning "little arms" (at prayer). From this word, the Germans derived the word *bretzel*, which came into English as *pretzel*. Another story insists that the term comes from the Latin *pretiola*, which means "little reward," because the legendary originator of the treat gave the breads to children as rewards for reciting their prayers.

Whatever their precise origin may be, it's a great idea to enjoy some pretzels during the Lenten season — and let them remind us to pray!

— *PT*

Q. What are gargoyles, and why are they found on churches?

A. A *gargoyle* is a waterspout (usually made of stone) that projects from a roof gutter or upper part of a building to throw water clear of walls or foundations. It minimizes water erosion. The term is derived (as is the word "gargle") from the French *gargouille*, meaning "throat."

Some gargoyles are undecorated, but the memorable ones — most popular in the Gothic-style churches of the Middle Ages — are carved into fanciful, often grotesque, shapes. They may portray humans, beasts, human-beast hybrids, animal hybrids (*chimeras*), or demons. By extension, any similar figure adorning a building has come to be called a gargoyle. But technically, if it's not a waterspout, it should be called a *grotesque*, not a *gargoyle*.

We don't really know for sure why medieval churches were adorned with these bizarre-looking characters. Scholars have suggested various theories:

- They reminded churchgoers that the enemies of their souls lurk outside the holy place, ready to tempt them to sin.
- They were intimidating "guardians" designed to frighten away demons.
- They were pre-Christian pagan symbols, "baptized" for Christian use.

- They were whimsical or mischievous, a form of medieval humor.
- The vulgar ones may have been carved as retribution for mistreating the stone carver.

— PT

Q. What is the holiday known as "Twelfth Night"?

A. In most of the Western Church, the "Twelve Days of Christmas" are the twelve days beginning with Christmas Day itself and concluding with the vigil of Epiphany on the traditional calendar. (The traditional observance of Epiphany was on January 6, so January 5 would be the last of the twelve days.) Epiphany, of course, honors the visit of the Wise Men (also called "Magi" or "Kings") to worship the baby Jesus (see Mt 2:1-12).

In some traditions, the "Twelve Days of Christmas" begin instead on the evening of December 25, with the following day, December 26, considered the "First Day" of Christmas. In these traditions, the twelve days thus include Epiphany itself (January 6).

The merrymaking celebration called "Twelfth Night" (that is, the twelfth night of the Twelve Days of Christmas) traditionally took place throughout parts of Western Europe on the evening of January 5, the vigil of Epiphany. It was observed by feasting, plays, and all kinds of tomfoolery. Some of its distinctive customs apparently had their roots in celebrations that pre-dated the coming of the Christian faith to that area of the world.

The customary fare for Twelfth Night feasting in England featured "wassail," an ale-based drink mixed with honey and spices. It was served in large bowls passed among family members and friends with the greeting "Wassail!" which comes from the old English phrase "*Waes hael*," meaning "Be well!"

Also important for Twelfth Night celebrations was the "Kings' Cake," in honor of the visit of the "Kings" who came to worship Our Lord. A bean, coin, or little figure of the Christ Child was baked into the cake, and then slices of the cake were distributed. Whoever found the object in his or her piece was chosen to rule as "king" or "queen" over the festivities. Since the Mardi Gras season traditionally begins with Epiphany, this cake became part of those celebrations in French homes, including those in the Gulf Coast region of the U.S.

Incidentally, William Shakespeare's play *Twelfth Night, Or What You Will* (written c. 1601) was written to be performed on this holiday.

— PT

Q. What are "Ember Days"?

A. Ember Days (in Latin, *Quattuor Tempora*, "four times") are the days at the beginning of the four seasons formerly prescribed by the Church as days of fasting, abstinence, and prayer. Christians also were encouraged to receive the sacrament of Penance on those days.

The origins of Ember Days are somewhat obscure. Pope St. Leo the Great (d. 461) considered them an apostolic tradition, but they also seem to have corresponded to ancient pagan ceremonies (Roman, or perhaps Celtic) that called on agricultural gods for help in times of harvest and seeding. Perhaps, given her well-known strategy of sanctifying popular practices by reinterpreting and reorienting them according to the Christian faith, that's why the ancient Church at Rome established these fasts in June, September, and December. In the beginning, the exact days weren't fixed but were announced by the priests.

By the third century, Ember Days were fixed at Rome by Church law; by the fifth century, the celebration of a fourth season was included. Ember days also became a time for the ordination of priests and deacons, which had formerly been reserved to Easter.

After the fifth century, the practice of Ember Days spread from Rome throughout Western Europe, though it never took hold in the Christian East. Pope St. Gregory VII (c. 1021-1085) prescribed them for the entire Church on the Wednesday, Friday, and Saturday after Ash Wednesday, Pentecost Sunday, the Feast of the Exaltation of the Holy Cross (September 14), and St. Lucy's Day (December 13).

The 1969 *General Norms for the Liturgical Year* describe Ember Days as times when "the practice of the Church is to offer prayers to the Lord for the needs of all people, especially for the productivity of the earth and for human labor, and to give Him public thanks" (N. 45). The local conference of bishops is to determine "the time and plan of their celebration" (N. 46).

— *PT*

Q. What are "Rogation Days"? In the traditional Church calendar, several days had that notation.

A. In the traditional Church calendar, Rogation Days were certain prescribed days of fasting and prayer in the spring, associated with intercession especially for the harvest, but also asking God's mercy and blessings in general. (The name comes from the Latin *rogare*, "to ask.")

The "Major Rogation," on April 25, adapted to Christian purposes the pagan practice (called *Robigalia*) of holding processions through the cornfields to pray that the crops would be preserved from mildew.

The "Minor Rogations" were kept on the Monday, Tuesday, and Wednesday before Ascension Day. These rogations were derived from processional litanies established by St. Mamertus of Vienne (c. 470) to pray for relief from the volcanic eruptions that plagued his diocese. They eventually spread throughout the Roman province of Gaul, then to Rome and beyond.

The liturgical reforms adopted after 1970 officially eliminated Rogation Days from the Church calendar. But with the recent *motu proprio* of Pope Benedict XVI allowing for a wider use of older liturgical forms, many Catholics are rediscovering this ancient tradition.

— *PT*

Q. Did St. Francis really write the famous "Prayer of St. Francis"? I recently read that the popular prayer beginning with the words, "Lord, make me an instrument of your peace," did not actually originate with him. Is that true? If not, how did it come to be attributed to Francis?

A. Though the prayer is typically attributed to St. Francis, it is almost certainly a modern creation. Historians came to this conclusion some time ago, but recently the Vatican's newspaper, *L'Osservatore Romano,* raised the issue anew when it reported that the prayer first appeared in France at the start of the twentieth century and became popular during World War I.

The prayer was first published, in French, in a Catholic weekly newspaper in 1912. Also known as the "Simple Prayer," it was then republished on the front page of the Vatican newspaper in 1916 at the request of Pope Benedict XV. The Holy Father especially liked its message of peace in the midst of World War I.

The actual author remains anonymous. So why was the prayer attributed to Francis?

Historians note that it's inspired by Franciscan themes, but the language is not typical of thirteenth-century Italian, which Francis spoke. There doesn't seem to have been any organized attempt by anyone to deceive people into believing that Francis was the author. Perhaps it was later attributed to him because it was made popular by a French Franciscan between the two World Wars, who printed it on cards with an image of Francis on the back.

— *PT*

Q. Are religious tracts a Catholic invention? I often find a fundamentalist religious tract on the windshield when I return to my car after shopping at the mall.

A. St. Francis de Sales (1567-1622) pioneered the strategy of doing Catholic evangelization and apologetics by leaving little slips of paper with short handwritten sermons in places where people could find and read them.

St. Francis was a French priest, and in his day, tens of thousands of Catholics in French-speaking Switzerland had fallen into the Calvinist heresy. So he went there to become a missionary, hoping to win them back to the Catholic faith. The reception was icy, to say the least; he was known to sleep in haylofts and even trees, even during the bitter winters, because almost no one would let him in the door of their homes, much less give him a night's lodging. People often threw rocks at him.

Nevertheless, St. Francis persevered. He realized that many people were probably interested in what he had to say, but they were afraid to be seen by their neighbors listening to his preaching. So he devised a plan. He wrote out his sermons on little leaflets and slipped them under the doors of homes at night when no one could see him. When the residents found them, they could read his sermons privately without fear of spying neighbors. Eventually, St. Francis had the leaflets printed and was able to distribute them openly and post them publicly. You could say, then, that these were the first religious tracts.

Through his perseverance, St. Francis enjoyed considerable success. Estimates of how many people he helped return to the Catholic Church range from 40,000 to 72,000.

St. Francis became both a bishop and a Doctor of the Church.

— *PT*

Q. What is the significance of blessing lambs on St. Agnes' feast day? I recently heard that Benedict XVI did this.

A. In this traditional ceremony, the pope blesses two live lambs presented by the nuns of the convent of St. Agnes in Rome. The lambs' wool is then used to weave a *pallium* (plural, *pallia*) for each of the new metropolitan archbishops, which will be presented to them by the Holy Father on June 29, the Solemnity of Sts. Peter and Paul.

The pallium, in its present form, is a white circular band, "three fingers wide," embroidered with six black crosses. It's worn over the chasuble around the neck, chest, and shoulders; and has two pendants, one hanging down in front and one behind. The pallium is worn by the pope and by metropolitan archbishops as a symbol of ecclesiastical authority and the special bond between the bishops and the Pontiff.

— *PT*

Q. What's an antipope?

A. An antipope is someone who makes a false claim to be the pope, based on a process of election, installment, or even self-appointment that is contrary to the Church's laws. Historians typically recognize as antipopes only those false claimants with a significant following, such as large numbers of the faithful, powerful political backing, or some portion of the college of cardinals.

Lists of antipopes compiled by scholars vary because questions have arisen in particular cases over how to harmonize historical criteria with those of theology and canon law. The *Annuario Pontificio* (*Pontifical Yearbook*), the annual directory of the Holy See, lists thirty-seven antipopes, beginning with Hippolytus — whose false claim to St. Peter's throne lasted from 217 to 235 — and ending with Felix V (1439-1449).

Antipopes in the early Church were typically promoted by rival ecclesiastical parties in Rome. In later centuries, they were more often puppets of secular rulers attempting to undermine or co-opt papal power. A few, however, had broad enough international support within the Church itself to become serious rivals to the popes they opposed. There are actually a few people today who claim to be the true pontiff in opposition to Pope Benedict XVI, but none of them has a substantial enough following to be included in the Church's list.

— *PT*

Q. Has there ever been a pope who formally taught heresy?

A. No pope has ever formally taught heresy. Anti-Catholic apologists claim that Pope Honorius (625-638) taught heresy and was condemned by the sixth ecumenical council in 681. This claim arises out of a misunderstanding or a misrepresentation of the facts.

Here are the facts. Following the teaching of Pope Leo I, the Council of Chalcedon in 451 decreed that Jesus Christ is fully human and fully divine. Large groups in the East rejected this formula, mistakenly believing it denied the unity of Christ's nature. In the next two centuries, numerous attempts were made to reconcile those groups to the Catholic Church.

In 619, Sergius, patriarch of Constantinople, offered a compromise formula. He taught that while Christ did have two complete natures, he had only a single will. This formula, called *monothelitism* (from the Greek word for "one will"), immediately became the cause of widespread controversy in the East. The popes of the time had no information about this formula and the controversies it had engendered.

In 634, Sergius wrote a cleverly worded letter to Pope Honorius, seeking to enlist the Pope's support in his cause. Sergius said that he would be willing to withdraw his theory of "one will" in Christ if others would stop insisting on the Chalcedonian formula of two natures in Christ. The Pope should have known that if Christ did not have a human will, he could not have been human, but only divine. Sergius' doctrine should have been condemned outright, and the Chalcedonian formula reaffirmed.

Instead, through ignorance of the issues and through carelessness, Pope Honorius agreed it would be wise not to debate the issue of one or two wills in Christ. He rightly said there could be no opposition of wills in Christ because Christ always did the will of the Father. And that is all Pope Honorius said in reply to Sergius' inquiry.

Note that the pope was not proclaiming a rule of faith; he was only urging silence on the issue. His reply to Sergius was communicated to only a few Eastern bishops. The bishops of the West knew nothing of Pope Honorius' letter to Sergius.

When the sixth ecumenical council condemned monothelitism and its adherents in 681, they included Pope Honorius among those condemned. Recall now that the decrees of all the ecumenical councils were always submitted to the pope for his approval and promulgation. Conciliar decrees had no effect until the incumbent Pope promulgated them, and only in the terms by which he confirmed them.

When the sixth ecumenical council's decrees were submitted to Pope Leo II, he confirmed them. At the same time, however, he made it clear that Pope Honorius was not condemned for teaching heresy but for failing to condemn the monothelite heresy when it was first brought to his attention.

Anti-Catholic apologists also contend that, until the eleventh century, the oath that Roman pontiffs took before their enthronement included a condemnation of Pope Honorius. What those apologists fail to see — or choose to conceal — is the fact that throughout those four centuries succeeding the incident, popes condemned Pope Honorius not for teaching heresy but for failure to condemn it when it first was brought to his attention.

— *RR*

Q. How did the custom of popes choosing new names arise? May they use their own birth name?

A. First, some background: the earliest popes did not choose a different name once they took the papal throne. The first to do so was Pope John II (died 535). A Roman by birth, he was named Mercurius, after the Roman god Mercury; he took the Christian name John because he thought a pagan name would be a dishonor to the papal office. Pope John III (died 574) may also have changed his name, but we don't know for sure.

In the latter part of the tenth century, four more popes chose new names for themselves upon ascending the throne, and the custom was firmly established by the middle of the eleventh century.

The choice of name belongs to the pope himself. Thus, although there is no canon law requiring that someone take a different name upon becoming Pope, the tradition now has the weight of centuries behind it. In addition, the practice has a certain usefulness, since it allows each new Pope to make a kind of statement about his hopes and intentions for his papacy.

Reasons for the names chosen have varied. Popes John II and John III apparently took that name to honor their martyr predecessor, Pope St. John I. When a German named Bruno was named Pope in 996, he probably took the name Gregory V as a way to reassure the Romans that even though he was a "foreigner," he would serve them just as faithfully as earlier, Italian popes had done.

In our own day, Blessed John XXIII and Paul VI were the popes who presided over the Second Vatican Council. As a way of honoring them and associating themselves with the work of that council, Paul's successor took the name John Paul (the first instance of a pope taking a double name), and John Paul's successor chose to be called John Paul II.

Pope Benedict XVI probably took that name for several reasons. St. Benedict (c. 480-c. 547) is the patron protector of Europe, and this pontiff seems especially concerned about that continent's threatened spiritual welfare. He has also spoken of the need for the Church to be a creative spiritual minority within the world, as the Benedictine and other religious orders have been. Also, the previous Benedict was a peacemaker, as this Benedict hopes to be.

One interesting note: a Roman named Peter was elected Pope in 1009, but he changed his name to Sergius IV. His reason? Since the first Pope, St. Peter, held a unique position as the

"Prince of the Apostles," Sergius thought there should not be a "Pope Peter II."

To this day, the name Peter has never been taken by another pope.

— PT

Q. Are the prophecies of St. Malachy genuine? The claim is that they were written by an Irish saint in the twelfth century and make predictions about every future Pope up to the present.

A. The "Prophecies of Malachy" were alleged visions of the celebrated Irish saint Malachy O'Morgair, Archbishop of Armagh (d. 1148), received while he was in Rome in 1139 to consult with Pope Innocent II. They claim to provide what we might call predictive "mottoes" for every future Pope from Celestine II (reigned 1143-1144) to the last Pope, "Peter the Roman." The mottoes give a clue about the men or their time period.

St. Malachy allegedly gave his manuscript to Innocent II. It was then placed in the Roman archives and forgotten for four centuries.

Most reputable historians agree that the "Prophecies of Malachy" were, in fact, not written by St. Malachy, nor even by one of his twelfth-century contemporaries. According to Claude-François Menestrier, a respected seventeenth-century Jesuit scholar, the prophecies were fabricated around 1590. Their purpose was to influence a papal conclave that year by including a motto for the next Pope that would clearly apply to a particular papal candidate.

The list of papal mottoes was first published five years later by a Benedictine monk, resulting in fierce debate over whether they were genuine. More than four centuries later, the fascination with them continues.

Why the skepticism among scholars? Historians offer several reasons:

- All attempts to locate the original manuscript have failed.
- The lapse of four centuries between St. Malachy's life-time and the "discovery" of the prophecies has no explanation, and the timing of their discovery — right when they could influence the 1590 conclave — is suspicious.
- The papal mottoes up until the time of the 1590 conclave are quite accurate, while most of those afterward are quite obscure and could easily be interpreted in varying ways (much like the "prophecies" of Nostradamus). In some cases, rather tortured explanations are required to apply the descriptions to the historical figures they supposedly predict.
- The life of St. Malachy is well documented, largely through a biography written by his good friend St. Bernard of Clairvaux. The biography makes no mention of his supposed papal visions, despite other claims that Malachy sometimes manifested a prophetic gift.

So what is it about the "prophecies" that continues to fascinate so many Catholics? Perhaps the best explanation is that a handful of the later mottoes actually do seem accurate.

For example, the Latin phrase for Pope Pius VII was *"Aquila Rapax"* ("rapacious eagle"). This has often been interpreted as a reference to Napoleon Bonaparte, the ruthless French emperor who was this Pope's nemesis and whose symbol was the eagle.

The motto for Blessed Pope John XXIII, *"Pastor et Nauta"* ("pastor and sailor"), was also on target. He was a great pastor and a former patriarch of the maritime city of Venice.

The motto for Pope John Paul II was *"De Labore Solis* ("sun in labor" or "sun eclipsed"). That pontiff was born during a solar eclipse.

Gloria Olivae ("glory of the olive") would be the motto for our current pope. The olive branch is an ancient sign of peace. Joseph Ratzinger, some say, took the name Benedict XVI because he wanted to emulate the peacemaking pontiff Benedict XV, to bring the world an olive branch. A second connection: the olive is also a symbol of one branch of the Order of St. Benedict (sometimes known as the Olivetans).

The most famous prediction on the list is the last. The final Pope, "Peter the Roman" (*Petrus Romanus*), "will feed his flock among many tribulations; after which the seven-hilled city will be destroyed and the dreadful Judge will judge the people."

These final words were not actually included in the original text published in 1595; that list concluded with Benedict's motto. They appear for the first time in a document published in 1820. Ironically, then, the most spectacular claim of the prophecies was not even part of the original version.

— PT

Q. Who were the first Christian converts in America?

A. Long before Jamestown was settled in 1607, Catholic missionaries from Spain were spreading throughout what is now the southeastern region of the United States. They preached the Gospel, baptized native converts to the Faith, and provided them with the sacraments and Christian catechesis.

Jesuits and Franciscans came to St. Augustine, Florida, the oldest continuously occupied settlement of European origin in the United States, founded in 1565. (This was forty-two years before the English colonized Jamestown and fifty-five years before the Pilgrims landed at Plymouth Rock.) From there they went out to establish missions in what is now Florida, Georgia, Alabama, and the Carolinas — nearly two centuries before the better-known Franciscan missions of the American southwest.

— PT

Q. Is it true that the first American Thanksgiving was actually held by Catholics in Florida, rather than Puritans in Massachusetts?

A. We might say that the feast that should be recognized as the first "Thanksgiving" in the European colonies of America actually occurred on September 8, 1565, in St. Augustine, Florida — 56 years before the English Pilgrims had their feast in Massachusetts.

The leader of the Catholic Spanish colonists, Pedro Menendez de Aviles, along with 800 Spanish settlers, celebrated a Mass of Thanksgiving and then invited the native Seloy tribe, who occupied the site, to join them for a grand meal. They probably feasted on the food items that had been stocked on their ship for the long voyage: *cocido*, a stew made from salted pork, garbanzo beans, and garlic; plus hard sea biscuits, and red wine. If the Seloys contributed food to the meal, then the menu might have also included wild turkey, venison, gopher, tortoise, mullet, corn, beans, and squash.

Even before the event in St. Augustine, numerous Masses of Thanksgiving for a safe voyage and landing had been held in Florida by priests with Spanish explorers such as Juan Ponce de Leon (in 1513 and 1521); Panfilo de Narvaez (1528); Hernando de Soto (1529); Father Luis Cancer de Barbastro (1549); and Tristan de Luna (1559). So, yes, the first "Thanksgiving" was actually held by Catholics in Florida.

— PT

7.

Questions about Moral Issues

Q. What are the "Seven Deadly Sins"?

A. The "Seven Deadly Sins" are more accurately known as the "Seven Capital Vices." A vice differs from a sin in that it's a sinful *habit*, a repeated act that causes a kind of "rut" in the soul inclining us to fall into that particular sin more and more. These particular vices are called "capital" (from the Latin word for "head") because they are — so to speak — the "fountainhead" vices from which others flow. They are pride, covetousness (or avarice or greed), lust, anger (or "wrath"), gluttony, envy, and sloth.

Note that not all anger is sinful; there is such a thing as "righteous anger," such as the kind Jesus sometimes demonstrated (see Lk 19:45-46). Anger only becomes sinful under certain conditions, such as when it is unjustified or out of proportion to the offense.

Covetousness differs from envy in that the former is an inordinate love of possessions, while the latter is a sadness or resentment over another person's good — his possessions, relationships, fame, popularity, power, or whatever.

Sloth is not mere laziness, but rather the unwillingness to "pay the price," so to speak, of doing what is right and good — the cost of holiness. The motto of the slothful: "It's just too much trouble for me to be good."

— PT

Q. How can any of us make a "perfect act of contrition"? We humans are finite beings, and as such we are limited in our understanding of the nature of God. Although we are able

195

to regret deeply that our human weakness and frailties have led us to violate God's laws with the understanding that these sins are an offence to God, how is it possible to understand this perfectly? If we cannot, then how can any contrition we offer be perfect?

A. The phrase "perfect contrition" does make us wonder. Who among us can do anything that is "perfect"?

The Church distinguishes between "perfect" and "imperfect" contrition. Both are gifts of God, bestowed on us by the Holy Spirit. The distinction is based not on the quality of our performance of contrition, but on the motivation of our contrition.

If our contrition "arises from a love by which God is loved above all else, contrition is called 'perfect'" (*CCC* 1452). "Perfect" contrition grants remission of venial sins. It also brings forgiveness of mortal sin, if one also firmly resolves to go to confession at the earliest opportunity.

"Imperfect contrition" (also known as "attrition") arises out of lesser motivations, such as revulsion at the hideousness of sin or fear of being eternally damned. This latter contrition does not bring remission of mortal sin, but it does dispose one to seek sacramental absolution.

The first part of the well-known "Act of Contrition" summarizes perfect contrition:

> O my God, I am heartily sorry for having offended Thee, and I detest all my sins because of thy just punishments, but *most of all because they offend Thee, my God*, who art all good and deserving of all my love.

> (emphasis added)

> — *RR*

Q. Can our conscience ever mislead us? We have always been taught one must follow his conscience. But consciences are not always correctly formed. Their guidance can be wrong.

If my conscience tells me to do something — or allows me
to do something — which, objectively speaking, is wrong,
am I still bound by my conscience?

A. The Catholic Church teaches that we must follow our
conscience. That simply means we must always do what we truly
believe is right and good. But the Church does not stop with
enjoining the following of conscience. The Church teaches with
equal emphasis that we must correctly *form* our consciences. That
is, we must ground them in the Church's moral and doctrinal
teaching.

Both correct and incorrect judgments of conscience bind us,
but in quite different ways.

The judgment of a correct conscience binds us absolutely. To
go against it would be sin. An incorrect conscience binds us only
incidentally, and on condition that we change it if we learn the
truth in the matter concerned.

Consider two points emphasized by Pope Benedict XVI in
his teaching on conscience. The fact that one must follow even an
erroneous conscience, he noted, "does not signify a canonization
of subjectivity."

Moreover, [though one must follow even an erroneous con-
science]:

> ... It can very well be wrong to have come to such skewed
> convictions in the first place. The guilt lies then in a dif-
> ferent place, much deeper — not in the present act, not in
> the present judgment of conscience, but in the neglect of
> my being that made me deaf to the internal promptings of
> truth. For this reason, criminals of conviction like Hitler
> and Stalin are guilty.
>
> — *On Conscience* (Ignatius Press, 2007), p. 38

In an ironic vein (he must have smiled when he wrote this),
the Holy Father pointed out:

It is strange that some theologians have difficulty accepting the precise and limited doctrine of papal infallibility, but see no problem in granting de facto infallibility to everyone who has a conscience.

— *Ibid.*, p. 59

— *RR*

Q. Is the use of Viagra wrong? I work at a rehabilitation hospital as a secretary with a doctor who cares for spinal-cord-injured patients. Often the doctor asks me to call a prescription into the pharmacy. When it comes to Viagra, my conscience bothers me, as I feel that some patients may not be married. I think about the immorality of it. What if some woman gets pregnant and decides to have an abortion? Would I be an accessory to this situation? Is it sinful on my part?

A. Given your position as the secretary for a doctor treating spinal-cord injuries, you would not be an accessory to an abortion. But you are wrestling with the problem of cooperation in evil — and listening to your conscience. Your conscience is alerting you to stand up for the truth in the workplace and thereby give effective witness to Christ.

Many good Catholics find themselves in these tricky situations. In this case, the scenario of an abortion is so far removed from your action of phoning in a prescription that the principle of double effect, which guides us when a good act has both a good and bad effect, should not even be considered.

The next question is whether the use of Viagra is intrinsically evil. (An intrinsically evil act is one that is sinful no matter why you do it.) If an action is intrinsically evil, you can never cooperate with it, even if it is the lesser of two evils. Simply put, the end never justifies the means.

The notion of an intrinsic evil act is a very important concept for the correct formation of conscience, and it is dealt with at length in Pope John Paul II's encyclical *Veritatis Splendor* (*The Splendor of Truth*, 1993). Echoing the teaching of Vatican II, that encyclical lists — among other intrinsically evil actions — abortion, murder, euthanasia, and contraception (see N. 80).

The use of Viagra is not intrinsically evil. It can be used legitimately to treat a medical problem. So you can call the pharmacy and order it for your patients. Still, it's clear from the wild promotion of this medicine that it can be taken for less-than-virtuous reasons.

If Viagra is prescribed to treat impotence, then it is only legitimately prescribed for men who are married. At this writing, there are no other known uses for it, though other possibilities are being researched.

What is your responsibility in this case as the secretary? If you know the person is not married and intends to use the drug to treat sexual problems, you should disapprove. But ordinarily, you will not know that information. You could take the matter up with the doctor and tell him or her clearly that you do not want to be part of a structure that condones or facilitates illicit behavior. Such an initiative could lead to fruitful discussions and perhaps a change of heart on the part of the physician, especially if you are an excellent and valued employee in every other regard.

— *FH*

Q. When are we to judge and when are we to refrain from judgment? The Bible tells us "we must not judge" but certain behaviors are clearly against God's will and involve grave sin. Must we really refrain from any moral evaluation of a particular behavior or way of life?

A. It's true that in the Gospel, Jesus says: "Judge not, that you be not judged" (Mt 7:1). St. Paul also rebuked certain Christians with the question: "Why then do you judge your brother?" (Rom

14:10). Nevertheless, in the Gospel we're told that Jesus also commands us to "judge justly" (Jn 7:24).

Our Lord didn't contradict himself here. There are actually different kinds of judgment, some of which we're to avoid, and some of which we're to practice. The New Testament Greek word (*krino*) — most often translated by the English verb "judge" — can have several meanings, including: distinguish between things, criticize or find fault with, decide, condemn a criminal, or dictate the punishment of a wrongdoer.

So in which sense are we to judge, and in which are we to refrain from judging? When we consider the contexts of the verses just cited, we find clues.

Jesus went on to say:

> "For as you judge, so will you be judged, and the measure with which you measure will be measured out to you. Why do you notice the splinter in your brother's eye, but do not perceive the wooden beam in your own eye?"

> — Mt 7:2-3, NAB

Our Lord is not saying here that we are never to make any kind of negative moral evaluation of behavior. If that were the case, He would have sinned against His own command, since He often rendered a negative judgment on actions and attitudes. In fact, if that were the case, the listeners He was rebuking could rightly have fired back at Him, "Hey, man — don't judge us!"

Rather, Jesus is saying here that we must not criticize or find fault with others by using stricter standards for them than for ourselves. The kind of person He's addressing here is not simply someone who criticizes. He's rebuking the "hypocrite" (Mt 7:5). I think He's also implying here that people who make a habit of criticizing — those for whom criticism is a "default mode" — are the ones most likely to be focused on the petty faults of others while neglecting weightier problems of their own.

The context of St. Paul's remark is also instructive. He asks, "Why then do you judge your brother?" and continues, "Why do you look down on your brother? For we shall all stand before the judgment seat of God" (Rom 14:10).

St. Paul isn't saying we can never come to a conclusion about whether a behavior is wrong and should be avoided. Instead, he's saying that we must avoid the kind of pride that causes us to "look down on" others because of their behavior, thinking of ourselves too highly because we aren't like them.

In fact, the passage leading up to the apostle's remarks shows that he was dealing with a particular group of people: those who "despised" their Christian brothers and sisters because of "disputes over opinions" about whether certain Jewish laws were still to be observed — a matter that was still open to debate among faithful Christians of the time (Rom 14:1, 3). We can't view this apostolic instruction, then, as some kind of blanket ban on rendering moral evaluations of behavior.

When St. Paul goes on to remind us that we will all stand before the judgment seat of Christ, he's warning us that even if we judge a behavior, we must not *condemn the person* committing it (vv. 10-12). In other words, we must not presume to dictate how the person is to be punished by God, or what kind of final standing the person will have with God.

This insight is confirmed by St. Luke's report of Jesus' warning about "judging": "Judge not, and you will not be judged, condemn not, and you will not be condemned" (Lk 6:37).

Why is this kind of judgment forbidden to us? The answer is simple: we are competent to judge (evaluate, conclude, decide) *only* those things that are *manifest* to us — for example, certain kinds of behavior that clearly contradict the Church's moral standards, given by God.

On the other hand, we are *not* competent to judge (discern and evaluate) things that are hidden from us: the interior secrets of a person's heart and mind, such as unspoken motivations; the weight of a person's past experience in shaping present behavior; the final outcome of a person's destiny in eternity. Only God knows these things.

As an example, let's take a situation in which the "we mustn't judge" platitude is often misapplied by Catholics: the evaluation of homosexual behavior. Sacred Scripture and Tradition, as consistently interpreted by the Sacred Magisterium of the Church, judge homosexual behavior as gravely immoral. Catholics are justified, then, in affirming this judgment when necessary. Neither Jesus nor St. Paul nor any other biblical passage can be reasonably cited to the contrary.

Nevertheless, with regard to individuals engaged in homosexual behaviors, some things are hidden to us that prevent us from passing certain kinds of judgment. We can't know all the factors in an individual's past that have contributed to the homosexual inclination or that might make it more difficult to resist temptation: childhood abuse or trauma; incorrect formation of conscience through misinformation; perhaps even biological factors (though research about the possible influence of biology is still inconclusive).

We also can't know the secrets of the individual's heart, such as the extent to which the orientation has been consciously chosen, or how great an effort of will is being exercised to resist temptation.

Finally, we can't presume to judge the individual's eternal destiny. Because we don't know the other hidden aspects of the situation, we can't know the degree of culpability. And we certainly can't predict what changes might take place in a person's life before he or she dies and appears before the Lord in judgment.

With regard to such "hidden" matters, St. Paul puts it this way:

> I do not even judge myself. I am not aware of anything against myself, but I am not thereby acquitted. It is the Lord who judges me. Therefore do not pronounce judgment before the time, before the Lord comes, who will bring to light the things now hidden in darkness and will

disclose the purposes of the heart. Then every man will receive his commendation from God.

— 1 Cor 4:3-5

— *PT*

Q. Are daydreams frowned upon by the Church? My friend said daydreaming is considered a sin because we are wishing for more than what God has given us.

A. It all depends what you mean by daydreaming, and the degree of consent given to such fantasies. If the daydream is about something sinful, and we consent to the thought, that would be a sinful thought. If the daydream is about something virtuous, or morally neutral, it could only be sinful if it were a waste of time, which it usually is. It is better for us to sanctify the moment and live in the moment, rather than wasting our time and energy dreaming about a future that might never come.

— *FH*

Q. What does the Church teach about putting animals "to sleep"?

A. The Church allows you to put your pets "to sleep" because God has given man dominion over the animals. While pets don't have rational immortal souls, they do have life and exhibit emotions and some level of knowledge and recognition. Pets respond to our commands and can provide services to us. Good pets in some way reflect God's goodness and can bring us companionship and joy.

Thank God for pets and take good care of them, in the spirit of St. Francis of Assisi. It should go without saying that we must never abuse animals in any way. At the same time, however, remember that pets are only animals and don't deserve to be treated better than humans, especially the unborn.

— *FH*

Q. What is the Church's stand on being an organ donor?

A. It is fine, even praiseworthy, for you to donate a non-vital organ in order to help someone recover health. While you are alive, however, you cannot donate a vital organ such as your heart (which would, of course, result in your death), although you could donate the second kidney or part of your liver.

However, as this topic is discussed and debated today, there are many other considerations that potential donors should know about.

First, the issue of organ transplants — and this is directly connected to organ donations — is addressed succinctly in the *Catechism of the Catholic Church* (2296). A couple of principles need to be kept in mind here:

1. Organ donation is acceptable only if the donor has given his informed consent.

2. While you are alive, you can donate only a non-vital organ.

If the donor has died, all organs can be donated. However, the current debate focuses on what constitutes death, and medical experts disagree about how to define "brain death" in particular.

I think the most prudent course of action is not to allow the "harvesting" of vital organs from a human body until brain activity, respiration, and circulation have all ceased: no breathing, no heartbeat, no blood pressure, and no brain activity.

Such a restrictive definition of death can cause a problem for those engaged in the organ-transplant business, as it is medically preferable to remove a vital organ from a body with a heartbeat rather than from a dead body. However, caution and prudence should prevail, as there are documented cases of surgeons removing vital organs from accident victims before it was certain they were dead.

— FH

Q. What does the Church teach about the disposal of "surplus eggs" from *in vitro* fertility procedures?

A. If only eggs are frozen, they can be disposed without further problem or ethical concern. But it's likely the physician has inventoried "fertilized eggs" — that is, human embryos — and human embryos are living human beings. So welcome to the brave new world in which tiny human beings are kept in a state of frozen suspended animation!

For this reason and for others, the Church condemned the practice of *in vitro* fertilization in the instruction *Donum Vitae* of February 22, 1987. The Church subsequently reiterated the condemnation in the *Catechism* (see *CCC* 2376-77) and in John Paul II's encyclical *The Gospel of Life* (*Evangelium Vitae*, 1995).

There seem to be four ways to treat the embryos, but not all of them are ethical:

1. Use them for research. This is clearly wrong because it constitutes the direct killing of human life. No matter how good the intention of the research, this would always be wrong.

2. Do nothing and eventually they will die (they deteriorate even while frozen). This seems unsatisfactory.

3. Thaw them, let them die, and bury them. This also seems unsatisfactory, for all human life deserves to be cared for. As for the suggestion that they should all be given burial, this is problematic, too. How could it be moral or ethical to bury alive a living human being?

4. Implant them in the mother or in another woman willing to adopt the child and bring them to term. Implanting them in the mother is the best course of action at this point, but unlikely in many cases.

As for adoption and implantation, reputable, trustworthy, and orthodox moral theologians have different opinions about adoption of the embryos. Some believe that it could be ethical and even "heroic" to adopt a frozen embryo, although that would not be morally obligatory for anyone. Even so, the 2008 instruction from the Congregation for the Doctrine of the Faith, *Dignitas Personae*, observed:

It has also been proposed, solely in order to allow human beings to be born who are otherwise condemned to destruction, that there could be a form of "prenatal adoption." This proposal, praiseworthy with regard to the intention of respecting and defending human life, presents however various problems not dissimilar to those mentioned above [with regard to certain clearly illicit practices].

All things considered, it needs to be recognized that the thousands of abandoned embryos represent a situation of injustice which in fact cannot be resolved (N. 18).

Implantation (adopted or not) is not free of ethical concerns because it constitutes a material cooperation in the business of IVF, which is intrinsically evil in the first place, although the implantation could perhaps be allowed under the principle of double effect.

The only answer to this dilemma is to prohibit IVF. In the words of Bishop Elio Sgreccia, President of the Pontifical Academy of Life:

> The practice of *in-vitro* fertilization must be stopped. It only encourages the production of frozen embryos, and freezing embryos is utilitarianism without mercy. When you start a wrong procedure like this, any solution is wrong and sad.

> — *Catholic World Report*, May 2001

> — *FH*

Q. If human beings were to be cloned, would the clones have souls?

A. Identical twins have souls, so cloned human beings would also have souls. The Catholic Church teaches that the human soul is created immediately by God for each individual, and if He creates separate souls for identical twins who start out as one human organism, then He would no doubt do the same for clones.

Would it make a difference that they are artificially produced? The manipulation of human embryos in this way would certainly be immoral. But that doesn't mean the resulting children would somehow lack a soul. Today, many children have been artificially fertilized (through *in vitro* fertilization), and these children certainly have souls. So there's no reason to think that just because clones are artificially produced, God would not give them souls.

— *PT*

Q. Does the Sixth Commandment apply only to married persons? Or is any kind of sex outside of marriage a sin against the Sixth Commandment?

A. The *Catechism of the Catholic Church* states: "The tradition of the Church has understood the sixth commandment as encompassing the whole of human sexuality" (*CCC* 2336). In other words, it condemns as contrary to God's will not only "adultery" in the strict sense of the word, but all kinds of sexual unions outside the bonds of marriage.

Sacred Scripture also repeatedly condemns all forms of sexual impurity (see Mk 7:21-23; Gal 5:19-21; Eph 5:3; Col 3:5; and Rom 1:18-27).

— *FH*

Q. Is it wrong to date if you are divorced but don't have an annulment?

A. Divorce is very sad, but we have to deal with it. Until a person receives a declaration of nullity about their first marriage, they should not keep company with another person because, in the Church, "marriage enjoys the favor of the law." That means until there is an annulment, we presume the first marriage is valid. Objectively, then, dating while divorced but without an annulment is wrong.

This can be very difficult advice to give, and even more difficult to receive. But whenever I've counseled cases such as these, I

208 208   Catholic Answers to Catholic Questions

have firmly encouraged people to trust in the wisdom of the Church and choose the higher road. In every case, things have worked out splendidly because the persons in question showed humility and faith and trusted in God and the wisdom of the Church. They received annulments and are now happily married with children, and more importantly, very close to Jesus Christ. Trust in the Lord!

— *FH*

Q. If a Catholic couple confesses the sin of sterilization, will their penance require no further sexual relations?

A. This is an issue for many, many people today, but it really needs to be handled on a case-by-case basis. No one should ever be afraid of Confession. Fear, in this case, comes from the evil one and is a consequence of personal sin. Recall the episode of the original sin in Genesis 3 and the sad response of Adam to God: "I was afraid . . . and I hid myself" (Gen 3:10). We should never allow fear of God to make us try to hide from Him, because He is our Father and loves us always.

When we sin, God calls us to conversion through the voice of our conscience. But true conversion requires true contrition. If a thief repented of his theft, an unmistakable sign of contrition would be restitution of the stolen property to the owner. In the case of sterilization, an unmistakable sign of conversion would be the reversal of the operation.

However, this may not be possible for some people because of the cost or because of the opposition of one of the spouses. Even if the reversal is unsuccessful, the attempt at reversal is a sign of true contrition and that is what heals the soul. Nonetheless, the confessor should not mandate reversal of the sterilization in order to receive absolution, but he could suggest reversal if the case warrants it.

In other cases, the confessor could suggest that the couple refrain from sexual relations during those times when the woman would most likely be fertile, and in this way their behavior would model Natural Family Planning. Ultimately, it is the Lord who reads the human heart and He would know if the spouses were truly repentant.

Still, other cases could be more complicated. For instance, one spouse could be truly repentant of the sterilization while the other may still be opposed to more children. In that case, the cessation of intimate relations could put an undue strain on the marriage. It would not be prudent for the confessor to require no further sexual relations in this situation.

— FH

Q. Where does Scripture say that people should not live together before marriage?

A. The Greek New Testament word, translated into English as "fornication," "sexual immorality," or sometimes just "immorality" (*porneia* — from which we get the word "pornography"), refers sometimes to sexual relations between unmarried persons and sometimes to that kind of sexual activity as well as adultery. In either case, the term always includes the meaning of sexual relations between unmarried persons.

Given that definition, we can find cohabitation prohibited or condemned in a number of biblical passages (Mt 15:19; Mk 7:21; Acts 15:20, 29; 1 Cor 5:11; 6:9-10, 18-20; 7:1-2; 10:8; 2 Cor 12:21; Gal 5:19; Eph 5:3; Col 3:5-6; 1 Thess 4:3-8; and Rev 21:8, 22:15).

— PT

Q. Was the Catholic Church the first Christian church to say no to contraceptives?

A. The Catholic Church, from which all the other Christian traditions have ultimately sprung, has condemned the use of artificial contraceptives since ancient times. In that sense, I suppose you could say that the Catholic Church was the first of the Christian communions to do so.

However, condemnation of contraceptives is not a recent

development. Prior to 1930, nearly all Christian communions were firmly opposed to contraception. In that year, however, the Lambeth Conference of the Church of England changed its position to allow contraception when abstinence was deemed "impracticable." The (largely Protestant) Federal Council of Churches followed suit the next year and, in time, the major Protestant denominations began to fall in line one by one.

It's ironic, then, that today the Catholic Church is often seen by some non-Catholic Christians as unreasonable in rejecting artificial contraception. They fail to realize that their own denominations were once in firm agreement with the Catholic Church on this issue.

— PT

Q. Is the marriage consummated if a couple uses contraceptives from the time of the wedding? They are, after all, not giving themselves completely to one another.

A. The marriage is understood to be consummated if "the spouses have in a human manner engaged together in a conjugal act in itself apt for the generation of offspring" (Canon 1061). The use of contraceptives would voluntarily render the act inapt for the generation of offspring and, ergo, the marriage would not be consummated until they stopped using contraception. That is because the procreation of offspring is an end of marriage.

The mutual gift of self as husband and wife is not complete if it does not include the possibility of maternity or paternity since the unitive and procreative aspect of marriage is inseparable. However, even if the marriage is not considered to be consummated, it is still presumed to be valid.

— FH

Q. If a person is married before a judge, then has the marriage legally annulled in court, are they required to have that marriage annulled by the Church as well?

A. Ordinarily, a Catholic who marries before a civil judge has not married validly because he failed to follow the canonical form that ordinarily requires the presence of the parish priest and two witnesses (see Canon 1108). If the marriage before a judge was annulled by a civil court, the Catholic would not be required to have that marriage annulled by the Church.

However, if the Catholic wants to get married in the Church to a different person, the details of that first marriage would need to be explained to the competent Church authority in the course of a pre-nuptial questionnaire. If there were children from the first marriage, the Church would actively encourage the original spouses to reconcile and have their union blessed by the Church, since this would normally be the best for the children.

— *FH*

Q. Can divorced Catholics receive Communion?

A. The Church does not deny the Eucharist to all who are divorced, but rather to those who have attempted to remarry without first obtaining an annulment — that is, the Church's authoritative judgment and public recognition that the first attempt at marriage was, in fact, invalid.

Why does remarriage without an annulment present a barrier to receiving Communion? Because the Church must affirm, at Jesus' instruction, that a true marriage can be ended only by the death of one of the spouses. A civil divorce may provide safety, emotional relief, and other benefits, but if the marriage was valid in the first place, it remains a reality until one of the partners dies.

If a person applied for an annulment and the Church refused to grant one, then the authorities competent to judge the matter concluded that the original marriage is in fact valid. Since a person can't be validly married to two people at once, this means that the present relationship, though recognized as a "marriage" in the eyes of the secular authorities, is not truly a valid marriage.

If a couple is living as husband and wife (that is, having sexual relations), but are not, in fact, husband and wife, that is a matter of grave sin. And those who are living in grave sin (of this or any other kind) should not receive Communion; it's a desecration of the Lord's Body and Blood.

It is possible for a divorced and remarried Catholic without an annulment to begin receiving Communion again, after sacramental confession, if the couple agrees to live (and, in fact, begin living) as "brother and sister"; that is, without sexual relations.

It's a difficult situation, but the Church cannot simply disobey the clear teaching of her Lord, nor ignore the realities He has shown us about the nature of marriage. This is why Catholics need, now more than ever, straightforward preaching and personal counseling about what makes a valid marriage and about the futility of attempting to contract a second marriage if the original one has been judged by the Church as valid.

— PT

Q. **What is the Church's teaching on Catholics attending a humanist wedding service or a wedding in a registry office?**

A. The Church doesn't ask Catholics to refrain from attending weddings of those who aren't Catholic, even weddings of a secular nature or ones that involve only a civil ceremony. Civil marriages are presumed valid by the Church (apart from obvious impediments to validity, such as same-sex "marriages"), though they are not sacramental.

Problems do arise, however, when Catholics, who are obligated to obey the Church's moral teaching and precepts, have weddings that are contrary to Church law. Is the bride or groom who is engaging in such a ceremony a Catholic without proper dispensations? In that case, you must wrestle with the question of whether your attendance would seem to signify your approval. Also, the Church does not allow Catholics to act as formal witnesses (maid/matron of honor, best man) in such situations.

— FH

Q. Is there a statute of limitations on the presumptive death
    of a former spouse in order that the remaining spouse may
    obtain the Church's blessing on a second marriage?

A. No, there is not a statute of limitations on the presumptive
death of a spouse. However, Canon 1707 of the *Code of Canon
Law* addresses the situation when the former spouse cannot be
located and therefore it cannot be proven if he or she is dead or
alive.

> 1707.1: Whenever the death of a spouse cannot be proven
> by an authentic ecclesiastical or civil document, the other
> spouse is not regarded as free from the bond of marriage
> until the diocesan bishop has issued a declaration that
> death is presumed.

> 1707.2: The diocesan bishop can give the declaration men-
> tioned in [1707.1] only if, after making suitable investiga-
> tions, he has reached moral certainty concerning the death
> of the spouse from the depositions of witnesses, from hear-
> say and from other indications. The mere absence of the
> spouse, no matter for how long a period, is not sufficient.

> 1707.3: In uncertain and involved cases, the bishop is to
> consult the Apostolic See.

If you are in such a situation, contact your local bishop and
present him with your case. Ask him to issue a declaration that
the death of your first spouse is presumed. If the bishop thinks
your case has merit, he will issue such a declaration, and then you
are free to marry.

— *FH*

Q. Is it fair that homosexuals have no choice but to live in
    perpetual chastity? Heterosexuals have the option of chas-
    tity or marriage. It seems to me homosexuals have been

disadvantaged by a lack of choice in this regard and have a steeper slope to climb to achieve salvation. This strikes me as unfair and inconsistent with the love and compassion of God for mankind.

A. Let's start with the distinction between "chastity" and "continence." All persons are called by God to the virtue of chastity. One's state of life determines what form that virtue will take for oneself. Chastity for the single person and for a religious means continence and purity. For the married, chastity means purity in total fidelity and devotion to one's spouse.

Since in God's plan persons with same-sex attraction have only the option of purity and continence, you think this is "unfair," that it is "inconsistent" with what we know of God's love.

It may be true that, as you say, the person with same-sex attraction has "a steeper slope to climb" on the way to salvation. Your reasoning seems to be that if a person has a "steeper slope to climb" than someone else, that is "unfair" and "inconsistent" with God's love.

Your underlying assumption seems to be that everyone should have the same difficulty (or the same ease) in "climbing" to salvation. But there is nothing in God's revelation to support or even suggest that assumption. Each person is unique. Each path to salvation, though directed toward the same Lord, is unique.

Indeed, the path will be more difficult for some than for others. This is not because God plays favorites or because He chooses to be "inconsistent" and in His bestowal of love. Not at all.

Rather, God totally respects the unique gifts and background of each person. He seeks to work with each person in the context of that person's situation.

There are various theories about the origin of same-sex attraction, but there is absolutely no evidence that God actively intends for some persons to have same-sex attraction. Even so, the fact that God has allowed the condition to appear shows that He can somehow incorporate it into His overall plan for that person's life. A person with same-sex attraction must continually seek to cooperate with God in fulfilling that plan.

Meanwhile, keep in mind that it is demeaning to a person to assume that because he is so much the slave of his hormones it is impossible for him to live a chaste life.

— *RR*

Q. My same-sex-oriented son receives Holy Communion. What should I do? I disapprove of his sexual lifestyle, but I still have and want a close and warm relationship with him. If I do speak out and act with disapproval, I will estrange myself from him. This would be devastating to us both.

A. From what you have written, I judge that you clearly distinguish, as we all must, between the sinner and the sin. No matter how much we deplore and object to things our children may do, we still love them. Indeed, it is because we love them that we must oppose behavior that we know is wrong and detrimental to their welfare.

The matter of your son's receiving Holy Communion in his present state is serious. The Church teaches us that we must not receive Communion unless we are in a state of grace: no unconfessed mortal sin, no continuing attachment to venial sin.

Scripture gives clear warning about receiving Communion if one is not in a state of grace:

Whoever... eats the bread or drinks the cup of the Lord in an unworthy manner will be guilty of profaning the body and blood of the Lord.

Again:

For any one who eats and drinks without discerning the body eats and drinks judgment upon himself.

— 1 Cor 11:27, 29

"Discerning the body" means, among other things, coming to the Lord in true contrition and repentance.

In my opinion, it is your clear duty to warn your son that in his present state it is spiritually perilous for him to receive Communion. This is not to show disapproval of him as a person, but to point out the danger of his conduct.

In the process of raising him there must have been many occasions when you had to rescue him from what could have caused him harm, even great harm. That is exactly what you would be doing by urging him not to receive Communion. You can make it plain that you give him this warning only because you love him and want what's best for him.

Finally, before you and your husband discuss this matter with him, pray earnestly for the Holy Spirit to speak through you in offering this guidance to your son.

— *RR*

Q. If someone has a sexual dream during sleep, then wakes up to find that he has had a nocturnal emission, has he sinned?

A. No. He has not sinned, because while he slept, such action was not directly voluntary.

The only thing I suggest for someone to do in such occasions is to examine his conscience to determine whether this event was *indirectly voluntary* because, while awake, he willingly entertained unchaste thoughts or glances. That could be at least a venial sin and something to rectify in the future. If you do not archive it in your memory, you will not rehearse it in your dreams.

— *FH*

Q. Is viewing pornography on the Internet a sin if I don't become aroused?

A. If you deliberately view pornography on the Internet then you are in some way condoning the immoral and indecent behavior of the participants. Sadly, sometimes the subjects of pornography find themselves in desperate situations and must resort to this activity for gain or some derived sense of self-esteem. If you view it, you are contributing to the problem, even if you do not become aroused.

At the very least, and this is the case even if you do not recognize it, the deliberate viewing of pornography hardens your heart, confuses your conscience, deceives you toward living a double life, and makes you callous and insensitive about the dignity of others.

The *Catechism* states:

> Pornography . . . offends against chastity because it perverts the conjugal act, the intimate giving of spouses to each other. It does grave injury to the dignity of its participants (actors, vendors, the public), since each one becomes an object of base pleasure and illicit profit for others. It immerses all who are involved in the illusion of a fantasy world. It is a grave offense.

— *CCC* 2354

— *FH*

Q. If an elderly person in a nursing home refuses to eat anymore, so to end his miserable life as soon as possible, is this considered suicide?

A. In my experience, it is rare for an elderly sick person in a nursing home to refuse to eat anymore in an attempt "to end his miserable life as soon as possible." More common is the experience that an elderly person is tired of life, sick of being sick, tired of being lonely, and longs to see his Maker. Gradually, he or she loses the will to live, and as a consequence, loses any desire to eat. That's not suicide.

— *FH*

8.

Questions about Apologetics

Q. Why don't Catholics interpret the Bible literally? My Protestant friends say we don't.

A. Perhaps you should begin by asking for specific reasons why your Protestant friends make this claim. Also ask them, for example, whether they *literally* interpret John 6 ("*eat* my flesh, *drink* my blood") — and if not, why not.

It would be far more important, however, for you to explain to them how the Catholic Church does interpret Scripture. The Catechism of the Catholic Church explains that the Church has always concentrated both on the *literal* and the *spiritual* senses of Scripture (*CCC* 109-119).

There are three facets, or dimensions, to the spiritual sense of Scripture. One the Church calls the *allegorical* sense, in which we see events of the Old Testament, for example, prefiguring Jesus Christ and His mission of salvation. The common example given in the Catechism is that the Israelites' crossing of the Red Sea points to, is a sign of, Christian baptism.

Another is the *moral* (or *tropological*) sense, which leads us to act virtuously.

The third is the *anagogical* sense (from the Greek word for "leading up" or "leading on high"). This third sense involves seeing the eternal dimension of events recorded in Scripture, and letting that vision impel us on our way to heaven. The Catechism example is Scripture's pointing to the Church as a sign of the heavenly Jerusalem.

Remember that both the literal sense and these three spiritual senses can be properly understood only under the guidance of the Church, who is the divinely appointed custodian of revelation.

In chapter seven of his *Essay on the Development of Doctrine*, Cardinal John Henry Newman shows that, in the early Church, those persons who insisted on the literal interpretation alone invariably wound up in heresy. He reminds us that the school of Antioch, the foremost training center for literal interpretation in the early centuries, was "the very metropolis of heresy." Drawing on his vast knowledge of Church history, Cardinal Newman wrote:

> It may be almost laid down as an historical fact, that the mystical [what we call the spiritual] interpretation and orthodoxy will stand or fall together.

— RR

Q. Does every Christian belief have to be "proved from Scripture" to be valid? Whenever I talk to my evangelical Protestant friends about Catholic beliefs, they always throw at me the challenge: "Prove it from Scripture."

A. The next time you encounter this challenge, give your Protestant friends another challenge. Say to them, "Though your presupposition that all must be proved from Scripture is wrong, for the moment I will accept it. Now, prove to me from Scripture that I have to prove to you from Scripture everything we Catholics believe." It cannot be done. Nowhere does Scripture even intimate that everything the Church teaches has to be proved *from* Scripture.

Your friends may fall back on the only verse they can find — 2 Timothy 3:16. But what does it say? "All scripture is inspired by God and profitable for teaching, for reproof, for correction, and for training in righteousness." This verse says nothing about "proving" things from Scripture.

What does "inspired" mean? Orthodox Christians take it to

mean that Scripture is the inspired, infallible Word of God. But you can't prove *that* from Scripture.

You could ask your Protestant friends to prove to you from Scripture that the true Church is where the Word of God is rightly preached and the two sacraments rightly administered. (That's a common Protestant definition of the church, coming from Martin Luther.) Or prove to you from Scripture the doctrine of the Trinity: God in Three Persons. Or show you where in Scripture they even find the word "Trinity." They can't.

Someone once asked G. K. Chesterton what the Bible says about a particular subject. His reply was that the Bible doesn't "say" anything. You can't put the Bible in a witness chair, ask it questions, and expect to get answers, he said. It's like any other book in the sense that it has to be interpreted.

Turning from Chesterton, we have to say that leaving that interpretation up to the individual (as in Protestantism) has resulted in the formation of more than 25,000 separate denominations. The number of new denominations grows constantly because of private interpretation.

One more point. Protestants often appeal to something called "the pure word of God," apart from all interpretation. There is no such entity. Every individual interpreter necessarily relies on some tradition for his interpretation. Again, Scripture has to be interpreted.

Who is qualified (indeed, authorized) to make that interpretation? The private individual? Or the Church that Jesus Christ established and to which He entrusted His teaching authority? Tell your friends they have only these two choices.

— RR

Q. How early in Church history was Mass celebrated on Sundays? Isn't Sunday "the Lord's Day" due to the Resurrection?

A. The early Christians began meeting for worship on

Sundays instead of Saturdays because that was the day on which Jesus rose from the dead. They called it "the Lord's Day." Two early Christian writers who referred to Christians meeting on Sunday provide sufficient evidence that this change took place long before the Emperor Constantine became involved in Church affairs in the fourth century. One of them was St. Ignatius of Antioch. Writing not long after the composition of St. John's Gospel (sometime between the years 98 and 117), he declared: "We are no longer keeping the Sabbath, but the Lord's Day" (*Epistle to the Magnesians*, 9, 1).

The other writer was Eusebius of Caesarea (c. A.D. 263-339), who reported:

> The Word [Christ] has moved the feast of the Sabbath to the day on which the light was produced and has given us as an image of true repose, Sunday, the day of salvation, the first day of the light in which the Savior of the world, after completing all his work with men and after conquering death, crossed the threshold of heaven, surpassing the creation of the six days and receiving the blessed Sabbath and rest in God.

> *— Commentary on Psalm 91*

Another ancient text called the *Didache* (some scholars believe it's as old as some of the New Testament books, though other scholars would say it was written a few decades later) says that Christians should meet together on "the Lord's Day" to celebrate the Eucharist. And a document known as the *Epistle of Barnabas*, written about the year 130, plus a work by St. Justin Martyr, c. 155, make similar references but are even more explicit that the day is Sunday, not Saturday.

Of course, we also have the biblical evidence: St. Paul talks about how the first believers came together on the first day of the week (1 Cor 16:2), as does the book of Acts (20:7). The latter

notes that this day was when believers came to "break bread" —
how the early Christians described the Eucharist. The book of
Revelation also refers to "the Lord's Day" (Rev 1:10).

Not only was Our Lord Jesus raised from the dead on Sunday, the first day of the week (see Mt 18:1; Mk 16:9; Lk 24:1;
Jn 20:1, 19); all His recorded appearances after His resurrection
occurred on Sunday as well (see Jn 20:19, 26), including His last
recorded appearance, to St. John on the Isle of Patmos (see Rev
1:10). In addition, when Christ sent His promised Holy Spirit to
the Church on the Day of Pentecost, that, too, was a Sunday.

By choosing the first day of the week for His resurrection and
His post-resurrection appearances, not to mention the "birthday"
of the Church, Jesus Christ made the first day of the week forever
the "Lord's Day."

— PT

Q. Where is it in the Bible that we should ask the angels or Mary and the other saints who have passed on to pray for us?

A. When the Jewish general Judas Maccabeus was leading
the resistance to the Greek occupation of his country, he told
his soldiers about "a dream, a sort of vision, which was worthy
of belief" (2 Mac 15:11). In this vision, the general saw Onias, a
former high priest who had died, "praying with outstretched arms
for the whole Jewish community" (v. 12). Then he saw "God's
prophet Jeremiah, who loves his brethren and fervently prays for
his people and their holy city" (v. 14). In part, through the assistance of these two Old Testament saints, the Jewish fighters won
their battle.

The angel Raphael told the couple Tobit and Sarah, "When
you . . . prayed, I brought a reminder of your prayer before the
Holy One" (Tob 12:12). Then God sent Raphael to heal them in
answer to their prayer (v. 14).

The New Testament displays similar scenes. Jesus' parable of
Lazarus the beggar (Lk 16:19-31) assumes that the deceased man

is aware of those still living, is concerned with them, and wants to pray for them. In St. John's Revelation, the Christian martyrs in heaven knew what was happening on earth, and they prayed to God to accomplish justice there. In addition, both the saints and the angels in heaven brought to God's throne "the prayers of the saints" (Rev 6:9-11; 5:6-8; 8:3-4).

In such passages, we find the saints and angels mediating before God for believers on earth, either interceding or otherwise assisting them. (In the parable, even someone in hell is attempting to do so, if unsuccessfully.) Does this contradict St. Paul's statement that "there is one mediator between God and men, the man Christ Jesus" (1 Tim 2:5)? No, because the apostle wasn't excluding the participation of others in Christ's mediating role. In fact, whenever Christians pray for one another, whether in heaven or on earth, they are doing just that. In a similar way, Jesus is the "chief" Shepherd of His flock (Jn 10:11-16; 1 Pet 5:4), yet he assigns lesser shepherds to take part in this ministry (Jn 21:15-17; Eph 4:11).

Catholics ask the saints and angels for their help, then, for the same reason they ask Christians on earth to pray for them and assist them in other ways: it has pleased God to make us interdependent as members of Christ's Body (1 Cor 12:12-27).

— *PT*

Q. Is Easter a pagan holiday? I have some friends who insist that Catholics celebrate a pagan holiday of Easter! What can I say to justify our calling Resurrection Sunday by the name "Easter"?

A. The English *name* we use for the greatest of Christian feast days, "Easter" (and its cognate in German), may well have pagan roots. Scholars have long debated its origins, so we don't know for sure. But the festival *itself*— commemorating Our Lord's resurrection — is, of course, anything but pagan. Christians have observed it from the beginning as the holiest day of the year.

In other languages, Easter is typically called "Great Day" or "Resurrection Day" or, most often, some term derived from the Greek name, *Pascha*, which is itself derived from *Pesach*, the Hebrew festival of Passover. The connection between Easter and Passover should be clear, as St. Paul noted, "For Christ, our paschal [Passover] lamb, has been sacrificed. Let us, therefore, celebrate the festival" (1 Cor 5:7-8).

The Catholic Church has no inherent connection with the term "Easter," as is clear from the fact that most English-speaking Protestants use that term as well. In fact, references to the day in Catholic liturgy just as often call it the "Paschal feast."

If your friends feel uncomfortable calling a day by a name with a pagan derivation, then I suggest that they simply refer to Easter as "Pascha" or "Resurrection Day."

But I'm curious: if they have such strong objections to using pagan names for days, what do they call the days of the week? The English names for the days of the week — Monday, Tuesday, Wednesday, and all the rest — were named for pagan gods and goddesses. And what about our names for the months, some of which have similar derivations? If they object to the use of pagan-derived names but still use these common English names for days of the week and months of the year, they are being rather inconsistent.

— *PT*

Q. How should we respond to claims that the resurrection of Christ was just a hoax, hallucination, or superstition?

A. If we affirm the essential historical reliability of the Gospel accounts (and there are many good reasons to do so, even aside from the requirements of Christian faith), we must conclude that none of these suggested alternatives is plausible.

Three kinds of historical evidence confirm the reality of the event: the reality of the empty tomb; the post-Resurrection appearances of Christ to more than 500 witnesses; and the consequent faith and life of the apostles, who were convinced by those appearances that He was indeed alive.

First, the empty tomb. In itself it was not a direct proof of the Resurrection, since the absence of Christ's body from the tomb could be explained in other ways. Nevertheless, it was an essential sign for Christ's followers and a challenge to the skeptics. If the crucified body of Christ had remained in the tomb, there could have been no credible claims of a resurrected Lord; the enemies of the Gospel could simply have produced a dead body to quash the rumor. But they could not.

Second, we cannot discount the testimony of so many eye-witnesses as some kind of mass hallucination produced by shared faith expectations. Rather, "To them he presented himself after his passion by many proofs" (Acts 1:3). Consider:

- The encounters with the risen Christ occurred in a variety of times and places.
- The reported details of the encounters differ significantly, and the people who had the encounters were of various backgrounds, with differing dispositions toward belief (see Mt 28:9-10; Lk 24:13-49; Jn 20:11-30; 21:1-23; Acts 1:1-9; 1 Cor 15:3-8).
- Some of them actually touched His body and watched Him consume food they had given Him (Lk 24:36-43).
- Meanwhile, since their faith in Jesus had been shattered rather than confirmed by the crucifixion, many were startled or doubting when He appeared to them.

Taken together, these circumstances prevent us from reasonably concluding that we are dealing here with mass hallucination caused by ecstatic faith.

Third, the possibility of a hoax or conspiracy to cover up the truth is ruled out by the subsequent behavior of the apostles and other witnesses. They dedicated the rest of their lives to proclaiming that Christ had been raised from the dead, and they willingly endured imprisonment, torture, and even death for the sake of that declaration (see Mt 28:11-15; Acts 12:1-5). Is it reasonable to think that these men and women would be willing to live and die in this way for what they *knew* to be a lie?

Finally, as the scriptural account shows, first-century people were no more likely than we are to be superstitious or gullible about claims of returning from the grave. The apostles themselves reacted with skepticism, not to mention others (see Lk 24:9-11; Jn 20:24-25; Acts 17:32).

— *PT*

Q. Is it true that Jesus was only "spiritually" resurrected? The Jehovah's Witnesses and certain other religious groups teach that Jesus was not alive in His physical body.

A. The Gospel accounts show otherwise. The tomb was empty, and the disciples encountered Jesus alive in His physical body — the same body they themselves had laid there:

> And as they were saying this, Jesus himself stood among them, and said to them, "Peace to you." But they were startled and frightened and supposed that they saw a spirit. And he said to them, "Why are you troubled, and why do questionings rise in your hearts? See my hands and my feet, that it is I myself; handle me, and see; for a spirit has not flesh and bones as you see that I have." And when he had said this he showed them his hands and his feet. And while they still disbelieved for joy, and wondered, he said to them, "Have you anything here to eat?" They gave him a piece of broiled fish, and he took it and ate before them.

> — Lk 24:36-43

Clearly, then, Our Lord's entire human nature was resurrected — not just His spirit, but also His physical body. The *Catechism* concludes:

By means of touch and the sharing of a meal, the risen Jesus establishes direct contact with his disciples. He invites them in this way... to verify that the risen body in which he appears to them is the same body that had been tortured and crucified, for it still bears the traces of His passion (cf. Lk 24:30, 39-40, 41-43; Jn 20:20, 27; 21:9, 13-15).

— *CCC* 645

— *PT*

Q. Why do Catholics pray for the dead?

A. For Catholics, praying for the dead seems as natural as breathing. If we pray for loved ones while they are still on earth, why not continue to pray for them after they die? Nevertheless, most Protestant Christians don't pray for the faithful departed. They believe that immediately after death, you go directly to heaven or to hell. If you're in heaven, they conclude, you have no need of prayers. If you're in hell, prayers will do you no good. In short, they don't pray for the dead because they don't believe in *purgatory.*

What exactly is purgatory? According to the *Catechism of the Catholic Church*:

All who die in God's grace and friendship, but still imperfectly purified, are indeed assured of their eternal salvation; but after death they undergo purification, so as to achieve the holiness necessary to enter the joy of heaven. The Church gives the name *Purgatory* to this final purification.

— *CCC* 1030-1031

Before the dead in Christ can go to heaven, then, they must be purified. And our prayers can help them in that process.

Sacred Scripture and Tradition repeatedly affirm that God's ultimate intention is for us to become perfect, as He is perfect (see

Mt 5:48). Why? Because God wants us to live forever in friendship with Him, and He himself is completely holy — without sin or weakness of any kind. To see God face-to-face in heaven, and to know, love, and enjoy Him there fully forever, we must be like Him (see Heb 12:14; 1 Jn 3:2-3).

In fact, heaven simply wouldn't be *heaven* unless those who lived there had been perfected. If we were to bring along with us all the sins and weaknesses we have in this life, heaven would be just as full of troubles as our life on earth — troubles that would last for eternity.

Didn't Christ die to forgive us our sins and save us? Yes! But even those who, through His infinite merits, have escaped the penalty of hell — an eternity without God — find that sin has countless other consequences. It disorders our souls. It injures others. It leaves us overly attached to things we have chosen to love more than we love God.

If we are to live with God forever, then, repairs and reparations are necessary — that is, we must be healed, and we must make amends. If we're selfish, we must learn to love. If we're deceitful, we must learn to tell the truth. If we're addicted, we must break the addictions. And if we're bitter, we must forgive.

Suppose a driver injures himself and totals another person's car in a collision because of his willful recklessness. As the ambulance arrives at the hospital, he expresses remorse for his misbehavior. So the other driver forgives him — that is, the other driver chooses to let go of the personal offense and not hold it against him.

Yet other consequences of the reckless driver's sin must still be dealt with. His broken bones must be set. The wrecked cars must be paid for. His driver's license must be suspended until he successfully completes a course that trains drivers to be responsible.

The process will not be pleasant. Having broken bones set is painful. Paying for a wrecked car is costly. Learning to change lifelong habits is wearying. Even so, the process is restorative — a matter of both mercy (the repairs) and justice (the reparations). In the end, the reckless driver will be a new man.

The truth is that we've all wrecked our lives, and the lives of others, to one extent or another. Whether in this life or the next, however, God doesn't wave a magic wand, bypassing our free will, to fix the situation. Instead, we undergo a procedure to undo what we have done: paying our debts, letting go of whatever binds us, straightening out whatever is crooked within us, learning to drive aright.

Of course, this process has already begun in the lives of the faithful on earth. Through doing penance and accepting in faith the inescapable sufferings of the present life, we can be purged of sin's effects and grow in holiness.

Nevertheless, if we look honestly at those we know who have died — even if they were faithful Christians — we must admit that few, if any, seemed to be perfect when they left this world. They still needed, as we ourselves probably will, some "cleaning up," a painful but purging "fire," as Scripture calls it (see 1 Cor 3:14-15).

That's precisely why we pray and offer Masses for those in purgatory. Our intercession helps them in their struggles now just as it helped them while they were on earth. No wonder, then, that Scripture urges us not to forget the faithful departed: "For it is . . . a holy and wholesome thought to pray for the dead, that they may be loosed from sins" (2 Mac 12:46, Douay).

— PT

Q. Why does the Catholic Bible have seven more books than other Bibles?

A. Seven Old Testament books are found in Catholic Bibles but not in Protestant ones. Catholics call them the *deuterocanonical* (literally, "second canon") books; Protestants call them the *apocryphal* (literally, "hidden," thus "unknown, spurious") books. These books include Baruch, Tobit, Judith, 1 and 2 Maccabees, Wisdom (or Wisdom of Solomon), and Sirach (or Ecclesiasticus).

They were included in the *Septuagint*, a third-century-B.C. Greek translation of the Old Testament, which served as the Scripture of the apostles and the generations that followed them. The earliest Greek manuscripts of the Old Testament, such as *Codex Sinaiticus* (fourth century) and *Codex Alexandrinus* (c. 450), include the deuterocanonical books with the others.

Regional Church councils at Hippo (in the year 393) and Carthage (397 and 419) listed these books (and the other sixty-six) as Scripture, endorsing what had become the general belief of the universal Church. The ecumenical Council of Trent confirmed this canon in the sixteenth century.

How did Protestant Christians lose these books from their Bibles? The influential Protestant Reformer Martin Luther deleted them. Though he insisted that Scripture must be the sole authority for the Christian faith, when scriptural texts did not support his teaching, he tended to deny the authority of the books in which those texts were found.

The deuterocanonical books include passages that support the practice of offering prayers and sacrifices for the dead — and by extension, the doctrine of purgatory as well (see 2 Mac 12:39-45). Luther rejected this ancient teaching and practice of the Church, so he denied the deuterocanonical books a place in the Protestant canon. He also dismissed the New Testament book of James as an "epistle of straw" (though he left it in the Protestant canon) because it clearly teaches — contrary to Lutheran doctrine — that both faith and works are necessary for salvation (see Jas 2:14-26).

The books of the "second canon" are similar in style to other Old Testament books. Wisdom and Sirach are much like Proverbs. Tobit is in somewhat the same literary category as the book of Job. Judith is comparable to Esther (two heroic Hebrew women who helped save their people). First and Second Maccabees are historical narratives like the books of Kings and Chronicles. And Baruch is prophetic literature, akin to Jeremiah.

The New Testament closely reflects the thought of the deuterocanonical books in certain passages. For example, Revelation 1:4 and 8:3-4 appear to make reference to Tobit 12:15. St. Paul, in 1 Corinthians 15:29, seems to have 2 Maccabees 12:44 in mind; and Hebrews 11:35 mirrors the thought of 2 Maccabees 7:29.

— PT

Q. Why do Catholics call priests "Father" when Jesus taught we should "call no man father"?

A. Jesus did indeed say: "And call no man your father on earth, for you have one Father, who is in heaven" (Mt 23:9). In light of these words from the Gospel, many non-Catholic Christians object to Catholics calling priests "Father." So how do Catholics understand this passage?

In this situation, Jesus was rebuking the Pharisees for their spiritual pride (see Mt 23:2-10). He reminded them that God alone — God the Father — is ultimately the source of all authority, even the authority these men wielded within the religious community.

But was this simply an admonition to the proud, or did Jesus actually mean that under no circumstances are we ever to refer to anyone as "father"? Just consider: if the latter is true, then we could never legitimately speak of Church Fathers, or founding fathers of a country, or even biological fathers.

This could not have been Jesus' intent, however, given the words of Jesus on other occasions reported in the Gospels. The truth is that Our Lord himself used the term "father" numerous times to speak of someone other than God (for example, Mt 15:4-6; 19:5, 19, 29; 21:31; Jn 8:56). In telling the parable of the rich man and Lazarus, Jesus even had Lazarus use the title "Father Abraham" three times to refer to the patriarch of ancient Israel (Lk 16:24, 27, 30).

Later on, St. Paul certainly had no qualms about calling himself a "father" to other Christians (Phil 2:22; 1 Cor 4:15).

Interestingly enough, Jesus gave another warning immediately before he cautioned his disciples about the word "father":

> "But you are not to be called rabbi, for you have one teacher, and you are all brethren."

> — Mt 23:8

The word *rabbi,* in Jesus' native tongue of Aramaic, means "teacher." Do those who object to calling priests "father" refrain from calling anyone "teacher" as well?

Jesus himself spoke of teachers (Mt 10:24-25; Lk 6:40; Jn 3:10). St. Paul called himself a teacher (1 Tim 2:7; 2 Tim 1:11) and noted that teachers are, in fact, one of the ministries God has set in the Church (1 Cor 12:28-29; Eph 4:11). Any Bible concordance will reveal many other occurrences of the words "father," "fathers," "teacher," and "teachers" throughout Scripture.

Clearly, then, Jesus was not forbidding any use of the word "father" or "teacher." As the Catholic tradition has always understood, the correct interpretation of this command — and of every biblical passage — must be discovered in light of the Scripture as a whole.

> — PT

Q. The Bible says Jesus had "brothers and sisters," so why does the Catholic Church say He was an only child?

A. This question is often raised. The problem for English translators of Sacred Scripture is that ancient languages such as Hebrew and Greek did not clearly distinguish different kinds or degrees of kinship.

"Brother" or "sister" was used to designate all of the same family or clan. The word "brother" is also used in the New Testament to designate a member of the Church. In both Old and New Testaments — especially the Old — "brother" is frequently used as a synonym for "person" or "human being."

We read in Matthew 13:55-56 the names of certain "brothers" of Jesus: James, Joseph, Simon, and Judas. Yet Matthew 27:56 tells us that James and Joseph were sons of a Mary other than the Virgin. Presumably, Simon and Judas also were not children of the Virgin.

That's why, strictly on the basis of Scripture, it is not possible to say exactly what the terms "brother" or "sister" mean when used in connection with Jesus. For a correct understanding, we have to rely on the teaching of the Church that produced the Scriptures as a compendium of her Tradition. From the beginning, the Church has always taught that the Virgin bore only one child, our Savior.

One further consideration: if Mary had other children, why did Jesus, with His dying breath, entrust her into the care of someone not belonging to their family? In that culture, had she other children, it would have been a deep insult — a betrayal of family loyalty — for Jesus to give her into the care of St. John.

— RR

Q. My husband is a member of the Latter-day Saints (the Mormons). How do I reply to Mormons when they ask why we don't baptize the dead in light of 1 Corinthians? "Otherwise, what do people mean by being baptized on behalf of the dead? If the dead are not raised at all, why are people baptized on their behalf?" (1 Cor 15:29).

A. Bible scholars have long debated what St. Paul meant by this statement. Some believe that such a practice existed in the church at Corinth when the apostle wrote to them, but that it wasn't licit. In this case, his reference does not imply his approval of it, but is simply part of his argument for the certainty of the Resurrection. He was pressing the point that the people at Corinth must implicitly believe in the Resurrection if they have such a custom.

If this first interpretation is correct, the practice apparently persisted in some places, especially among certain heretical groups (the Cerinthians and the Marcionites, according to Sts. Epiphanius and John Chrysostom), because it was finally banned by two fourth-century Church councils (Council of Hippo, 393; Third Council of Carthage, 397).

Other scholars think that "the dead," though plural in the Greek text, referred to Christ, and so could be translated this way: "Why are you baptized for [one of] the dead [that is, Jesus], if the dead are not raised at all?"

— PT

Q. I was confronted by a non-Catholic Christian who said that I don't have to confess to a priest my sins and that Jesus denounced it in the Bible. Why do Catholics confess their sins to a priest?

A. Your inquiry raises two issues.

First, the friend's claim that Jesus denounced confession: not only did Jesus not denounce it, He commanded it. Ask your friend to read again Matthew 16:19, which records Jesus' bestowing on Peter the powers of binding and loosing (sins), which include the power of absolution. Then turn to Matthew 18:18, where similar authority is given to the apostles. Finally, look at John 20:22-23, the record of another bestowal of powers of absolution on the apostles, to "forgive" or "retain" sins. Jesus never dealt with options. He bestowed this power with the intention that it be used.

Now, why did Jesus institute Confession (the sacrament of Reconciliation)?

Think about the nature of sin. Sin, first of all, is an offense against God. We can and should confess our sins privately to God. But what assurance do we have that we have been forgiven?

Apart from the sacrament of Penance, our only assurance is our interpretation of words in Scripture. Foreseeing the human need for objective assurance, Jesus authorized His apostles, their successors, the bishops, and bishops' aids — priests — to give that assurance in His name.

But there's more. Sin is not only an offense against God. It also harms those around us. Even what we think of as purely private sins deeply affects us and, therefore, inevitably affects the fabric of our relationships with others.

Imagine yourself standing beside a quiet pond. You throw a good-sized rock out into the water. You watch those concentric circles go out and out from the point of impact. You can't see where all those circles go.

Sin is like that. We can never know who are all the persons affected adversely by our sin. We can never know how all have been harmed. We can never ask forgiveness of all those persons. Nevertheless, we need that forgiveness. That is why Jesus authorized certain persons to speak in behalf of the community we have harmed by our sin, giving us their forgiveness.

— RR

Q. **When did the Church and Catholics begin calling themselves "the Catholic Church" and "Catholics" as opposed to "the Christian Church" and "Christians"?**

A. The word "Catholic" is the English version of the Greek word *catholikos*, a combination of two Greek words meaning "throughout the whole." The word occurs often in the Greek classics, with the sense of "universal."

The first use of the phrase "Catholic Church" in surviving historical records comes from around the year 110. In his *Letter to the Smyrnaeans*, St. Ignatius of Antioch wrote, "Let no one do anything touching the Church, apart from the bishop.... Where the bishop appears, there let the people be, just as where Jesus Christ is, there is the Catholic Church" (n. 8). The usage of "Catholic" here seems to connote "one and only." The casual way in which Ignatius uses the phrase suggests it was familiar to those to whom he was writing. If that was true, then it must have been in circulation well before St. Ignatius used the term in the generation immediately after the apostles.

Certainly by the beginning of the third century, the word "Catholic" as applied to the Church denoted that community which held sound doctrine, in contrast to heresy, and which was united in organization, in contrast to schismatic groups. The word also connoted wholeness, in contrast to the partial. In the writings of St. Cyprian (mid-third century), we see the beginning of using "Catholic" and "Roman" interchangeably.

The word "catholic" does mean literally "universal," but it means a great deal more. It connotes the fullness of the Faith. Early heretical and schismatic groups distorted the Faith by clinging to some parts and blowing them out of all proportion. The Catholic Church alone proclaimed the fullness of God's revelation. In fact, it was while addressing the issue of schism that St. Ignatius used the term "Catholic" to distinguish the Church from those who had broken away from her.

That is still true today. The word "Catholic" connotes wholeness. Simply to call the Catholic Church "Christian" (which indeed she is!) would not distinguish her from those many thousands of denominations who hold to a part of the Gospel, while neglecting or denying other and essential parts.

— *RR*

Q. Why do we call Mary the "Mother of God"? My friends who aren't Catholic say it sounds as if she has existed eternally and gave birth to God the Father.

A. To understand, we have to look first at Jesus. From the very beginning, the Church has proclaimed that Jesus Christ is both God and Man. Jesus claimed for himself the very name of God revealed to Moses, "I AM" (Jn 8:58), and He assumed divine prerogatives such as the forgiveness of sin (see Lk 5:18-26).

The apostles testified to this reality. St. Thomas, for example, having known Jesus in His humanity, affirmed His divinity as well when he said to Him after His resurrection, "My Lord and my God!" (Jn 20:28).

St. John wrote in his Gospel that Jesus was "the Word" who "became flesh and dwelt among us," and that this "Word was God" (Jn 1:1, 14). St. Paul taught that in Christ "the whole fulness of deity dwells bodily" (Col 2:9).

When early Christians pondered these and other declarations of the apostolic witness, they wondered how, exactly, was Christ both human and divine? Was He, as some claimed, simply God and only appeared to be human? Was He, as others speculated, a human to whom God attached himself in a special way, dwelling inside Him? Or was He, as still others imagined, a kind of hybrid, partly human and partly divine?

Ultimately, in the light of Scripture and Tradition, and led by the Holy Spirit, the Church concluded that none of the above answers is correct. The Council of Ephesus, an ecumenical Church council held in the year 431, helped to resolve the issue. That council was provoked by a controversy over one particular question: can we legitimately call Mary "the Mother of God"?

One prominent archbishop, Nestorius, began to preach against the use of the Marian title *Theotokos*, which means literally "God-bearer," or "the one who gives birth to God." Christ was two persons, he claimed — one human, one divine — joined together in Christ. Though Mary was the bearer (or mother) of the human person in Christ, she was not the mother of the divine Person (God the Son). So she could not rightly be called the Mother of God.

After examining this teaching, the Church pronounced Nestorius mistaken. Christ was not a combination of two persons, one human and one divine. That would be close to saying that He was simply a man to whom God was joined in a uniquely intimate way — a man specially indwelt by God, like one of the Old Testament prophets.

Instead, the Church declared, Christ is only one divine

Person — the Second Person of the Trinity. This single Person took our human nature and joined it to His own divine nature, so that He possesses two natures (Jn 1:1-3, 14).

But those natures don't constitute two different persons. Christ is not a committee. The two natures belong to one and the same Person, the divine Son of God. And those two natures, though not to be confused, cannot be separated.

In this light, the Church concluded that not only is it correct to call Mary the Mother of God; it's *important* to do so. Mary conceived and bore in her womb the one Person, Jesus Christ, who is God in the flesh. If we deny that she is the Mother of God, then we are denying that her Son, Christ himself, is God, come down from heaven.

For this reason, Catholics today follow the ancients in calling Mary *Theotokos*, "the God-bearer." The apostolic witness is clear: as St. Paul put it succinctly, "God sent His Son, born of a woman" (Gal 4:4).

— *PT*

Q. Is an act by Pope Julius II, which required the alleged purchase of indulgences, proof that papal infallibility does not exist? Can you please give me more information about this alleged act, and how to respond to this claim against papal infallibility?

A. This statement about Pope Julius II is false. He neither required nor approved the purchase of indulgences.

The facts are these. In 1517, Pope Julius II bestowed a plenary indulgence on all persons who went to confession, received the Eucharist, and made a contribution (any amount, according to what they could afford) toward the building of St. Peter's basilica. Johan Tetzel, a well-known Dominican priest, radically distorted the Church's teaching about indulgences by practically offering them for sale. He was immediately contradicted by Church authorities (Cardinal Cajetan, for one). What Tetzel

advocated would have been a clear case of simony (see Acts 8:18-
22), a serious sin.

— RR

Q. Has the Catholic Church tried to keep the Bible from the
   people? Frequently I read in Protestant sources that the
   Church has tried to keep the Bible in Latin, which is unintel-
   ligible to most Catholics, and that the Church has burned
   translations in the vernacular.

A. If the Church wanted to keep the Bible from her people,
why did Catholic bishops, priests, and laypeople keep copies of
the Bible safe — often at the cost of their lives — during the centuries of persecution, when Roman emperors decreed that all the
sacred books of the Christians should be burned?

Why did so many of the Catholic Church's monks spend
their lives making beautifully illustrated copies of Sacred Scripture? There was a scarcity of Bibles, since a monk working full
time might take a year to make one copy. Critics of the Church
condemn her for chaining copies of the Bible in churches. But
this was simply to protect against theft — Bibles were quite costly.

The Church's enemies often maintain that the Church has
opposed vernacular translations. So why did Pope St. Damasus
ask St. Jerome to translate the Bible from Greek and Hebrew into
Latin in the fifth century? To keep the common people from
reading it? Not exactly!

At the time, Latin was the language of the Roman Empire:
various peoples, from Britain to Persia, spoke it. But one of the
effects of the collapse of the Roman Empire was the loss of a
single unifying language. As a babble of local dialects sprang up
across Europe, Asia Minor, and North Africa, Latin became the
language of the schools, the professions such as law and medicine,
and, of course, the Church. So, well into the Middle Ages, Latin
was familiar to educated people who could read.

In Britain in the seventh century, before there was any English language, a monk named Caedmon rendered into the common tongue a paraphrase of a good portion of the Bible. In the following century, St. Bede translated some of the Bible into the then-common language.

In the ninth century, St. Cyril gave the Old Slavonic language an alphabet. Soon thereafter, St. Methodius translated the whole Bible into that language. In the ninth and tenth centuries, as well, appeared Anglo-Saxon translations of the Bible.

Scholars of the Church brought forth a number of Anglo-Norman translations after the Norman conquest of Britain in 1066. Then, of course, there appeared the great Douay-Rheims translation of the New Testament in 1582. The translation of the Old Testament followed in 1609.

In addition to vernacular translations in the British Isles, there were translations into other languages as well. By the time the Protestant movement began, popular translations of the Bible, or portions of it, existed in French, German, Spanish, Italian, and other European languages. The Church did not object to these translations.

Now, about the burning of Bibles. In the Middle Ages and later, it was customary to burn books that were regarded as erroneous. The Church did burn Bibles produced by John Wycliffe and William Tyndale, because the commentary contained in these Bibles, written by the translators, contained much heresy. The Protestant leader John Calvin also burned Bibles. He consigned to the flames a translation made by Michael Servetus, who was Unitarian. In fact, Calvin later had Servetus himself burned at the stake because of his heresy.

— *RR*

Q. What makes the "King James Bible" special? Some of my Protestant friends refer to it as if no other Bible version should be used.

A. Some Protestant believers do, indeed, insist that the "King

James Version" (KJV) of the Bible is the only legitimate English version. In fact, what Americans commonly call the "King James Version" is officially designated as the "Authorized Version." It was commissioned by the Protestant King James I of England and produced by 54 biblical scholars in 1611.

The text is a revision of the earlier "Bishops' Bible" (1568), rather than an original translation. But other previous English translations were consulted as well, such as the (Catholic) Rheims New Testament (1582), which had considerable influence on its language.

Though the Church of England had separated from Rome more than seven decades before, a battle still raged for its soul. More traditional believers, wishing to preserve many Catholic elements of faith and practice, defended the institution against the zeal of the more radical reformers, the Puritans in particular. Authorities responsible for the new version hoped to avoid these radical influences.

For that reason, they instructed the scholars to reject innovations the Puritans had made in religious terminology, such as replacing "baptism" with "washing" and "church" with "congregation." A close examination of the text shows that other more "Catholic" terms such as "bishop" (1 Tim 3:1) and "bishopric" (Acts 1:20) were also retained — no doubt to the chagrin of radical reformers who opposed the very notion of such an office.

The language of the KJV is quite beautiful and has exerted extensive influence on English literature and speech. Nevertheless, as the English language itself changed, and as scholarship in ancient languages and archaeology made new discoveries, Protestant authorities called for revised versions and new translations. One of the best known is the Revised Standard Version (RSV), published in the United States in 1946 and 1952, which was actually a revision of the KJV and also has two Catholic editions (1965, 2006) approved by the Church.

Protestants today who insist that the King James Bible is

the only legitimate English version of Scripture tend to view the Catholic Church unfavorably. So they might be startled to learn that the first edition of the KJV actually *included* the deuterocanonical books — that is, the books of the Catholic Bible that are lacking in present-day Protestant Bibles.

In addition, although many contemporary editions of the KJV include extensive commentaries presenting fundamentalist teachings, its devotees might be surprised to learn that such notes were originally banned from this version. The scholars were instructed to avoid sectarian ideas by including only the marginal notes necessary to explain certain Hebrew or Greek terms.

— PT

Q. I have a Protestant friend who insists that Catholic sacraments aren't biblical. Are the seven sacraments found in the Bible?

A. Yes, they are. There are too many references to quote them all in full here, but if you'll check out the following list of biblical texts, you'll find references, both direct and indirect, to all seven sacraments in the New Testament. Scripture may not name them explicitly using the name we have today (for example, Confirmation), but if you read the texts, you'll see that the sacrament is referred to there.

Baptism: Matthew 28:19; Mark 16:16; John 3:5; Acts 2:38; 16:15, 33; 18:8; 22:16; Romans 6:3-4; 1 Cor 1:11-17; 6:11; Colossians 2:11-13; Titus 3:5; 1 Peter 3:21.

Confirmation: Acts 8:14-19; 19:1-6; 2 Corinthians 1:21-22; Ephesians 1:13; Hebrews 6:1-2.

Eucharist: Matthew 26:26-28; Mark 14:22-24; Luke 22:19-20; John 6:47-58; 1 Corinthians 10:16; 11:23-30.

Reconciliation (also known as Confession or Penance): Matthew 16:19; 18:18; John 20:23; Acts 19:18; 1 Corinthians 5:3-5 with 2 Corinthians 2:6-11; 2 Corinthians 5:18-20; James 5:16; 1 John 1:8-9.

Anointing of the Sick (once known as Last Rites): Mark 6:5, 12-13; Luke 13:13; Acts 9:17-18; 1 Corinthians 12:9, 30; James 5:14-15.

Holy Orders (ordination of clergy): Matthew 18:18; Luke 10:16; 22:19; 24:45-49; Acts 1:26; 6:6; 15:2-6; 20:17, 28; 21:18; 1 Timothy 3:1-7; 4:14; 5:17; 2 Timothy 1:6; Titus 1:5-9; 1 Peter 5:1 (these texts include references to the act of ordination, to those who were ordained, and to the authority they received through ordination).

Matrimony: Matthew 5:31-32; 19:1-9; Mark 10:2-12; Luke 16:18; John 2:1-11; Romans 7:2-3; 1 Corinthians 7:1-24; 7:39; Ephesians 5:22-33; Hebrews 13:4; 1 Peter 3:1-7.

— PT

Q. My atheist friend insists that science has disproved the existence of miracles, and even my religion professor claims that the biblical stories about miracles are just legends or "figurative language." Isn't the existence of miracles a tenet of the Christian faith?

A. You are correct. Miracles belong to the very fabric of the biblical story from beginning to end. To dismiss them out of hand as impossible is to deny the foundations of the Christian faith. As St. Paul insisted, a Christianity without miracles such as the resurrection of Christ is no Christianity at all. It is "empty," "false," and in "vain" (1 Cor 15:12-19).

Some have indeed claimed that science has actually disproved the possibility of miracles. But consider Webster's dictionary definition of a "miracle":

An effect or extraordinary event in the physical world that surpasses all known human or natural powers and is ascribed to a supernatural cause.

Using that as a working definition, let's look closer at the claim.

Science attempts to construct an accurate picture of the natural world. Essential to its method are observation, hypothesis, and experimentation through controlled conditions. Given this goal and method, how exactly *would* science go about disproving the possibility of miracles?

On a given occasion, of course, scientists might well be able to demonstrate that an extraordinary event can be accounted for by purely natural causes. But how could they show that it is *impossible* for an event to have ever occurred in history that surpassed "all known human or natural powers" and had "a supernatural cause"?

First, scientists would have had to be present for observation at every event in history that has a claim to be miraculous. That is obviously not the case. Second, they would need a hypothesis that reasonably accounts for every such event that has ever occurred. They have no such hypothesis. Finally, if an event should actually have a cause *beyond* nature (supernatural), then the merely natural means at scientists' disposal would be incapable of observing it or controlling it for experimentation.

In short, science is too limited, in both scope and method, to *disprove* the possibility of miracles. On the other hand, science *is* often able to rule out *known* natural causes for certain extraordinary events. So the Catholic Church makes careful use of scientific methods when examining claims for contemporary miracles, such as those that appear in a cause for canonization — knowing that, since an almighty God exists, truly "nothing will be impossible" (Lk 1:37).

— *PT*

Q. How should we debate non-Catholic Christians and non-believers? As a convert, I feel called to share the Gospel because if I do not, then who will? On the other hand, I am a bit tired of debating with those who have so much animosity toward the Catholic Church.

A. My experience suggests that when someone is so thoroughly hostile to the Church, there's not much we can do at that point except pray for him or her. That's even more the case when the person has an emotional investment in us and has viewed our entering the Catholic Church as a personal betrayal. Attempts to debate in that environment lead only to deeper division.

This is not to say that unity is to be desired above truth. It's simply to say that the path to truth may for the moment be blocked by anger, confusion, and the sense of betrayal. The lenses of a person's intellectual "eyeglasses" are fogged up with emotion — not to mention the debris of misinformation that typically circulates about the Catholic Church.

I find that it helps to keep the big picture in mind: God will send along others to aid those who are sincerely seeking the truth. Your coming into the Church planted a seed inside some people. Now it will probably be the role of someone else to water the seed. If those to whom you speak cooperate with God's grace, someone else will most likely have the privilege of reaping the spiritual harvest (see St. Paul's remarks in 1 Corinthians 3:6-7).

In other words, the whole burden of testimony doesn't rest on you. The most important witness you could have given, you did, in fact, give: you entered the Catholic Church, despite the great personal sacrifices involved. Someone else may have to take it from there.

— PT

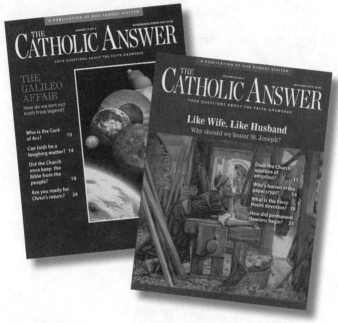